Organizing & Cleaning with ADHD

How Anyone Can Declutter, Manage Distractions, Build Routines, and Create a Stress-Free Home in Minutes a Day

Avery Holland

© **Copyright Avery Holland 2024 - All rights reserved.**

The content within this book may not be reproduced, duplicated or transmitted without direct written permission from the author or the publisher.

Under no circumstances will any blame or legal responsibility be held against the publisher, or author, for any damages, reparation, or monetary loss due to the information contained within this book. Either directly or indirectly. You are responsible for your own choices, actions, and results.

Legal Notice:

This book is copyright protected. This book is only for personal use. You cannot amend, distribute, sell, use, quote or paraphrase any part, of the content within this book, without the consent of the author or publisher.

Disclaimer Notice:

Please note the information contained within this document is for educational and entertainment purposes only. All effort has been expended to present accurate, up-to-date, and reliable, complete information. No warranties of any kind are declared or implied. Readers acknowledge that the author is not engaging in the rendering of legal, financial, medical or professional advice. The content within this book has been derived from various sources. Please consult a licensed professional before attempting any techniques outlined in this book.

By reading this document, the reader agrees that under no circumstances is the author responsible for any losses, direct or indirect, which are incurred as a result of the use of the information contained within this document, including, but not limited to, — errors, omissions, or inaccuracies.

Contents

BONUS VI

Introduction 1

1. Understanding the ADHD Mind 3
   1.1 The ADHD Brain: A Unique Perspective
   1.2 Executive Function and Its Impact on Organization
   1.3 Harnessing Hyperfocus for Effective Organizing
   1.4 Common ADHD Traits and Their Influence on Cleaning
   1.5 The Power of Acceptance: Turning ADHD into an Asset

2. Breaking Down Overwhelm 13
   2.1 Managing Energy Levels for Consistent Cleaning
   2.2 Tackling Decision Fatigue to Break Through Overwhelm
   2.3 Overcoming Perfectionism in Organizing

3. Emotional and Mental Well-Being 21
   3.1 Mindfulness Practices for Focused Cleaning
   3.2 Managing Anxiety During Organizing Efforts
   3.3 Letting Go: Tackling Emotional Attachments to Clutter
   3.4 Building Confidence Through Small Wins

4. ADHD-Friendly Time Management 28
   4.1 Timeboxing: Maximizing Focus and Efficiency

    4.2 Task Stacking: Grouping Tasks for Better Flow
    4.3 Managing Squirrel Moments: Staying on Track
    4.4 Handling Deadlines and Time Constraints with Ease

5. Building Sustainable Habits   39
    5.1 Turning Routines into Rituals for Consistency
    5.2 The Power of Visual Reminders in Habit Building
    5.3 Maintaining Motivation Through Habit Challenges
    5.4 Dealing with Setbacks: Resilience in Routine

6. Breaking Down Tasks into Manageable Steps   50
    6.1 Micro-Cleaning Sessions: Achieving More with Less
    6.2 Task Stacking for Maximum Efficiency
    6.3 Overcoming Procrastination with Brain Dumps

Make a Difference with Your Review   57
   Help Others Take the First Step

7. Room-by-Room Organization: Creating Calm from   59
   Chaos
    7.1 The Kitchen and Pantry: Streamlining the Heart of Your Home
    7.2 A Clutter-Free Living Room: Relaxation Meets Order
    7.3 Bedroom Bliss: Creating a Restful Retreat
    7.4 Streamlining Bathrooms: Easy Cleanup Routines
    7.5 Tackling the Home Office: Enhancing Productivity
    7.6 Laundry Room Logic: Tackling the Tumbles

8. Digital Declutter and Management   75
    8.1 Managing Digital Distractions: Focus in a Digital World
    8.2 Using Apps and Tools for ADHD-Friendly Organization
    8.3 Creating a Minimalist Digital Life

9. Gamification and Creative Approaches — 84
    9.1 Using Apps to Gamify Your Cleaning Routine
    9.2 Creative Organizing Techniques for ADHD Minds
    9.3 Reward Systems: Motivating Through Incentives
    9.4 Incorporating Music and Movement in Cleaning Routines

10. Engaging with Family and Support Networks — 92
    10.1 Collaborative Cleaning: Engaging Partners and Kids
    10.2 Creating a Harmonious Home: Setting Boundaries
    10.3 Finding External Support: Groups and Communities

11. Inspiration and Success Stories — 99
    11.1 Case Studies: Successful Organizing with ADHD
    11.2 Lessons Learned: Applying Strategies in Everyday Life
    11.3 Celebrating Success: Reflecting on Achievements

12. Practical Tools and Resources — 108
    12.1 Creating Your Personalized Planner System
    12.2 Visual Aids: Using Charts and Infographics
    12.3 DIY Organizing Tools: Cost-Effective Solutions
    12.4 Printable Resources for Continuous Motivation
    12.5 Building Your Support Network: Finding Help and Accountability
    12.6 Continuing Your Journey: Embracing a Lifetime of Organization

Conclusion — 116

Make a Difference with Your Review — 118
    Help Others Take the First Step

References — 120

FREE

Access Your **Free** Tools!

Scan this QR code to download exclusive printables designed to make life easier! Inside, you'll find a meal planner and a cleaning checklist, complete with a simple "how-to-use" guide. These tools are perfect for turning plans into action and creating a more organized, stress-free routine. Start your journey today!

Introduction

Have you ever felt buried under clutter and chaos, wondering if peace and order were possible with ADHD? If so, you're not alone. Many of us know the cycle all too well—determined attempts at organization followed by frustration as piles grow and to-do lists seem endless. Living with ADHD can make managing daily tasks feel like an uphill battle. The struggle is real and shared by countless individuals navigating similar challenges.

Research shows that adults with ADHD often face more significant difficulties in organizing and maintaining their living spaces. This isn't just a minor inconvenience; it can impact your mental well-being, relationships, and productivity. Studies reveal that clutter and disorganization can increase stress and anxiety. For anyone with ADHD, these feelings can be even more overwhelming. The need for practical, effective strategies is clear.

This book is here to help. Its main goal is to provide you with advanced, actionable resources tailored specifically for individuals with ADHD. You deserve a stress-free and organized home, a place where you can relax and thrive. This isn't about imposing rigid systems or unrealistic expectations. It's about finding what works for you and using that to create order in your life.

Let me share a bit about myself. I'm Avery, a parent to three energetic kids, so I know firsthand the demands of keeping a busy household running smoothly. Driven by a passion for understanding ADHD and its unique challenges, I've devoted myself to researching and developing practical, effective strategies. With both personal experience as a parent and a researcher, I'm equipped with insights to address these challenges in a way that truly works.

What sets this book apart is its approach. Unlike many other guides, this book goes beyond beginner-level techniques. It focuses on advanced strategies and ADHD-specific methods. It includes real-life applications that resonate with your experiences. You'll find tools like bullet points, infographics, and interactive exercises specifically crafted for the way the ADHD brains work. These features aim to keep your attention and make the learning process enjoyable.

This book respects your intelligence and experience. It doesn't offer overly simplistic or generic advice. Instead, it provides advanced strategies that acknowledge the complexity of your life and challenges. You won't find cookie-cutter solutions here; you'll find insights tailored to your needs.

The book is structured to guide you step-by-step. It covers key areas such as decluttering, managing distractions, building routines, and creating a stress-free home. Each chapter is designed to tackle specific organizational challenges. You'll gain practical advice and empathy at every turn, empowering you to transform your habits and improve your quality of life.

As you turn the pages, know this is more than just a book. It's an invitation to embark on a journey towards a more organized and peaceful home. Change is possible, and you're not alone. I promise to support you with practical guidance and encouragement every step of the way.

Let's take this journey together with confidence and determination. You have the power to create the environment you deserve. Let's get started.

Chapter 1

Understanding the ADHD Mind

You know those moments when you're determined to organize a space in your home but suddenly find yourself buried in a pile of forgotten items, unsure where to start? It's not just you. This experience resonates with many who navigate life with ADHD. It feels like a constant tug-of-war between intention and distraction. The truth is, these challenges aren't just habits to overcome; they are deeply rooted in the unique workings of the ADHD brain. Understanding these intricate workings is essential to finding solutions that truly fit your life. This chapter will explore the neurological aspects of ADHD, offering insight into why specific tasks can seem so daunting and providing a foundation for creating personalized strategies that align with your strengths.

1.1 The ADHD Brain: A Unique Perspective

The ADHD brain is uniquely wired, making attention and organization a challenge. Think of it as a bustling city where signals occasionally get crossed. This is the everyday reality for those with ADHD, where neurotransmitter imbalances, such as dopamine dysregulation, play a significant role. Dopamine is the neurotransmitter that helps regulate mood, attention, and learning. In the ADHD brain, this regulation often goes awry, leading to the restlessness and impulsivity many experience.

Structural differences in the brain also contribute to these challenges. Research shows that certain areas, such as the prefrontal cortex—responsible for planning and impulse control—are often smaller or less active in individuals with ADHD. These differences can make everyday tasks feel like monumental challenges.

Key Neurological Traits of ADHD:

- **Dopamine dysregulation:** Impacts attention, learning, and mood, often causing restlessness and impulsivity.

- **Structural brain differences:** Reduced activity in the prefrontal cortex affects planning and self-control.

- **Focus challenges:** Tasks requiring sustained attention, particularly tedious ones, can feel overwhelming.

These neurological traits often manifest in struggles to maintain focus, especially on mundane tasks. You might start the day with a clear plan, only to find that distractions have derailed your efforts by midday. Procrastination becomes an easy default, especially when faced with overwhelming organizing or cleaning tasks. Clutter piles up—not just in your physical space but in your mind—adding to the chaos. This isn't about willpower; it's about how your brain is wired. Recognizing these traits is the first step in developing strategies that work with, rather than against, the ADHD brain.

ADHD doesn't present itself the same way in everyone. Some people experience inattentiveness, struggling to stay focused and organized. Others may have a more hyperactive-impulsive presentation, marked by restlessness and impulsivity. These variations highlight the need for personalized solutions. Every individual's experience is distinct, requiring customized approaches that reflect their unique challenges and strengths. Self-awareness becomes a vital tool in this process. Reflecting on your ADHD traits can illuminate where your organizational hurdles lie. Journaling exercises and self-assessment tools can provide clarity, helping you identify patterns and areas needing attention.

Understanding how ADHD affects organizational habits fosters self-compassion and patience, allowing you to set realistic goals. This knowledge helps you craft personalized strategies tailored to your strengths and needs. Acknowledging that your brain works differently is empowering—it means finding ways to navigate challenges gracefully and confidently. By understanding your unique brain, you're equipping yourself with the tools to turn challenges into opportunities for growth and transformation.

1.2 Executive Function and Its Impact on Organization

Have you ever wondered why, some days, it feels impossible to keep track of even the simplest tasks? That might be your executive function at play. Think of executive function as the brain's command center, managing skills like planning, organization, and time management. It's like an orchestra conductor, ensuring all parts work harmoniously. For those with ADHD, this conductor sometimes finds keeping the orchestra in tune challenging. The critical components of executive function include inhibition control, which helps you resist distractions and impulses, and working memory, which lets you hold and manipulate information in your mind. These skills are crucial for organizing and managing tasks but can be challenging when ADHD is in the mix.

When executive function isn't firing on all cylinders, it can manifest in various ways. You've likely experienced the frustration of procrastination, the dread of starting a task that seems overwhelming. This isn't laziness; initiating tasks without the right cognitive cues is a real struggle. Forgetfulness is another common challenge. Misplacing items or forgetting appointments can feel like a daily battle. These issues don't just affect your ability to organize; they can also impact your confidence and stress levels. It's like trying to build a house without a blueprint—disorganized and overwhelming.

So, how can you support your executive function? Consider these practical tools:

- **Planners and calendars:** Offer a visual and tangible way to track tasks and deadlines.

- **Reminders and alarms:** Your own personal assistant to nudge you to help you stay on track.

- **Morning and evening routines:** Reduce decision fatigue and set a positive tone for the day.

- **Weekly planning sessions:** Help you set priorities and create realistic goals.

These tools, though simple, create a structure that aligns with your brain's needs. It's all about creating a framework that reduces chaos and gives you a sense of control.

Exercise: Creating Your Routine Blueprint

Take a moment to visualize your ideal day. Break it down into morning, afternoon, and evening segments. What tasks need to happen in each part? Write them down, then think about structuring these tasks into a routine. Consider using a planner to map out these segments, noting any alarms or reminders needed to keep you on track. Remember, this blueprint is flexible—adjust it as you learn what works best for you.

Incorporating these strategies isn't about forcing yourself into a rigid system but finding what complements your unique brain. With patience and practice, you can create an environment that supports both your executive function and your well-being.

1.3 Harnessing Hyperfocus for Effective Organizing

Hyperfocus—it's a term many with ADHD know well. It describes losing track of everything around you because you're deeply engrossed in a task. You might start researching a topic for what feels like minutes, only to realize hours have flown by. This intense focus can be both a blessing and a curse. On one hand, it allows for remarkable productivity and creativity.

On the other, it can lead to neglecting other responsibilities or forgetting to take breaks. To harness hyperfocus effectively, try the following:

How to Trigger Hyperfocus:

- Create a quiet, distraction-free environment.

- Use background music or white noise to maintain concentration.

- Set specific, clear goals for each session.

- Break tasks into smaller steps, such as organizing a single drawer instead of an entire closet.

Tasks That Benefit from Hyperfocus:

- Decluttering digital files, such as old documents or photos.

- Planning and color-coding personal schedules or meal prepping.

- Organizing a specific area, like a desk or bookshelf.

Harnessing hyperfocus is not just about productivity—it's also an opportunity for creativity and self-expression. While hyperfocus can help you power through organizing tasks, it's also a chance to approach them in ways that feel uniquely rewarding. Consider turning organizing sessions into something enjoyable by incorporating personal touches, like creating visually pleasing spaces or experimenting with color-coded systems that reflect your personality. Think of these sessions as a way to transform your environment into a space that supports your goals and inspires you daily.

Hyperfocus also offers an opportunity to build momentum. Once you complete one task, the sense of accomplishment can drive you to tackle the next. Start with a small project, like organizing the junk drawer in your kitchen or decluttering a single folder on your computer, and let that success propel you forward. Over time, these moments of intense focus can help you build new habits, reinforcing your ability to stay organized even outside periods of hyperfocus. The key is to harness this powerful state of mind as a tool for growth, using it to create systems that align with your strengths and make organizing an empowering, rather than overwhelming, experience. By approaching hyperfocus with intention and balance, you can turn it into a transformative force for creating lasting order and harmony in your life.

Interactive Element: Hyperfocus Planner

Create a Hyperfocus Planner for your organizing tasks. List the tasks that benefit from deep concentration, like decluttering digital files or organizing schedules. For each task, note the environment that best supports your focus. Then, set clear goals—what do you want to accomplish in this session? Finally, decide on break intervals and use a timer to remind you to pause. This planner becomes a tool to channel your hyperfocus productively, turning potential distractions into an ally in your quest for order.

Through understanding and intentional application, hyperfocus can be a transformative force. By recognizing its potential and learning to guide it, you can transform organizing from a daunting task into a rewarding experience.

1.4 Common ADHD Traits and Their Influence on Cleaning

Cleaning can often feel overwhelming, especially when ADHD is part of the equation. Traits like distractibility, impulsivity, and forgetfulness often interfere with maintaining a tidy home. **Here are some ways ADHD traits can impact cleaning:**

- **Distractibility:** Shifting between tasks without completing any.

- **Impulsivity:** Starting new projects while cleaning, leaving tasks unfinished.

- **Forgetfulness:** Misplacing cleaning supplies or leaving clutter behind.

These traits manifest in ways that make cleaning particularly challenging. Imagine tidying your desk, only to be sidetracked by a pile of unopened mail. This leads you to the kitchen, where you start reorganizing the pantry. Suddenly, you realize the desk remains untouched. Impulsive purchases can also contribute to clutter. You might find that an unplanned shopping spree leaves you with bags of items that don't have a designated place, adding to the disorder. This tendency to accumulate possessions without a plan for organization only exacerbates the existing clutter, turning a simple task into a monumental challenge.

Yet, there are strategies to navigate these challenges and bring order back into your home.

Strategies to Tackle Cleaning Challenges:

- Set designated cleaning times to build consistency.

- Use checklists to stay focused and track progress.

- Personalize cleaning routines based on your energy levels.

- Reward yourself for completing tasks, turning cleaning into a positive experience.

Personalization is essential for creating a cleaning routine that feels manageable and sustainable. By tailoring your approach to your unique energy levels and preferences, you can reduce the stress of tackling household tasks. For example, you might find mornings are ideal for high-energy activities like vacuuming, while evenings are better suited to low-effort tasks like folding laundry. The key is to experiment and adapt as needed. Pairing your efforts with small, meaningful rewards—whether it's enjoying a favorite snack or relaxing with a good book—can turn cleaning into a more positive and rewarding experience. With the right strategies and a personalized approach, you can transform cleaning from a daunting challenge into an achievable part of your routine.

Reflective Exercise: Your Personalized Cleaning Plan

Take a moment to reflect on your cleaning habits. What are the tasks you find most challenging? Identify two specific areas or tasks that tend to become overwhelming. Now, think about your typical day. When do you feel most focused or energized? Use this insight to create a flexible cleaning schedule that aligns with your natural rhythms. Write down a simple checklist for one of the areas you identified, and consider a small reward for completing it. This plan is your starting point—adjust it as needed to fit your preferences and lifestyle.

By recognizing these common ADHD traits and understanding their impact on cleaning, you can begin to craft strategies that work for you. It's about finding a balance and creating a space where you feel comfortable and in control without the stress of unrealistic expectations.

1.5 The Power of Acceptance: Turning ADHD into an Asset

Living with ADHD often feels like a constant tug-of-war between your intentions and your actions, a balancing act between what you plan to do and what gets accomplished. It's easy to fall into a cycle of self-criticism and frustration when things don't go as planned. But what if we flipped the script? Embracing ADHD, with all its quirks and challenges, can transform how you approach organization. By accepting ADHD as a part of who you are rather than a flaw to fix, you can begin to see its unique traits as tools rather than obstacles. This shift in perspective can reduce self-criticism and open the door to a more compassionate understanding of your needs. Embracing acceptance fosters greater self-belief and confidence, empowering you to tackle organizational tasks with a renewed sense of possibility.

ADHD has strengths that, when recognized, can be incredibly beneficial in organizing efforts. Take, for instance, the high-energy levels that many with ADHD experience. You can channel this natural zest into completing tasks with enthusiasm and vigor. Imagine turning a mundane chore into a mini workout session, using your energy to power through it. Then there's adaptability. The ability to adjust spontaneously to changing plans can be a significant asset. When a day doesn't go as expected, which, let's face it, often happens, your capacity to pivot and find new solutions becomes invaluable. Embracing these strengths means you can view ADHD not as an obstacle but as a partner in creating a more organized life.

Adopting a growth mindset can further enhance your organizational skills. It's about seeing these skills as improvable, not fixed. Instead of feeling defeated by setbacks, view them as opportunities to learn and grow. Set incremental, achievable goals that allow you to build confidence one step at a time. Celebrate small victories, like organizing a single drawer or completing a short task list. These successes, however small, reinforce your ability to make progress and foster a sense of accomplishment that propels you forward.

Real-life stories often provide the best inspiration. My cousin is a perfect example of how ADHD doesn't have to be a barrier to managing big, complex projects. For years, she struggled with the everyday details of life, often feeling overwhelmed by routine tasks. So, the idea of overseeing something as monumental as building a new home seemed almost impossible. Yet, when the opportunity arose to design her dream home, she discovered that her ADHD traits, like her keen attention to detail and knack for list-making, became her greatest strength. She planned every room with care, ensuring each had designated organizational spaces—a specific place for everything, from kitchen essentials to storage for exercise equipment and art supplies.

Throughout the project, she kept her focus on the smallest details, managing everything from the overall layout to selecting materials and perfecting the finishing touches. By leaning into her natural abilities and staying organized, she turned what could have been an overwhelming task into a personal triumph. This process wasn't just about building a house; it became a journey of self-trust and growth. It showed her that ADHD wasn't a hindrance but a unique asset, allowing her to create a space that reflected perfectly her vision, personality, and need for structure. Her story illustrates the power of embracing one's ADHD traits and turning them into tools for success, proving that with acceptance and adaptability, lasting and meaningful organizational improvements are possible.

Acceptance doesn't mean settling for less. It means recognizing the unique tools you have at your disposal and learning how to use them effectively. By focusing on your strengths and fostering a mindset open to growth, you can begin to see ADHD as an asset rather than a hindrance. This perspective can transform your organizational habits and improve your quality of life, making room for peace and productivity where chaos once reigned. Remember, the path forward is yours to create, filled with potential and possibility.

Chapter 2

Breaking Down Overwhelm

The feeling of overwhelm with ADHD is like standing at the base of a mountain, unsure where even to begin climbing. The trick? Stop looking at the whole mountain. Break it down into smaller, manageable pieces. Start with one step—just one. Maybe it's clearing a corner of the room or tackling one pile of papers. Remind yourself that progress doesn't have to be perfect; it just has to happen. Focusing on one task at a time shifts your attention from the intimidating big picture to something achievable. Those small steps gradually add up, and before you know it, you're moving forward.

But even when you break things down, figuring out what to tackle first can still feel overwhelming. That's where the Eisenhower Matrix comes in—a simple yet powerful tool to help you prioritize effectively. Named after Dwight D. Eisenhower, this method organizes tasks into four categories based on urgency and importance:

1. **Urgent and Important**: These are your top priorities—the tasks that require immediate attention and directly impact your goals. Think of deadlines or pressing issues.

2. **Important but Not Urgent**: These tasks contribute to your long-term goals but don't demand immediate action. Scheduling time for them ensures they aren't overlooked.

3. **Urgent but Not Important**: These tasks feel pressing but don't significantly impact your goals. Delegate them whenever possible to free up your time and energy.

4. **Neither Urgent nor Important**: These are the distractions—the tasks that don't add value. Eliminating or minimizing them can help you focus on what truly matters.

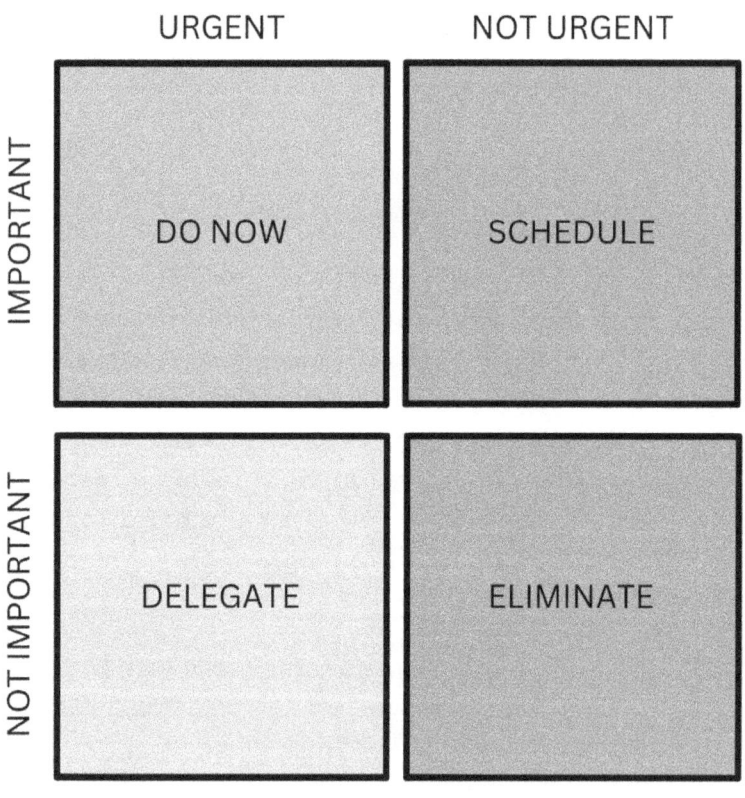

THE EISENHOWER MATRIX

By sorting your responsibilities into these categories, you can focus on what truly matters, reducing stress and creating a more manageable to-do list. This approach helps you avoid getting stuck in busy work and ensures your energy goes toward tasks that align with your long-term goals.

In addition to the Eisenhower Matrix, assessing tasks by their impact is another effective strategy. Begin by pinpointing tasks that will have the most significant impact on your daily life or long-term goals. These are the activities that will move the needle, the ones that make everything else easier or unnecessary. Once you've pinpointed these key tasks, you can allocate your time and energy accordingly. This method streamlines your workflow and ensures your efforts align with your priorities. It's about working smarter, not harder, and ensuring your actions are purpose-driven.

To practice prioritization, consider implementing daily and weekly planning sessions. Begin each day by writing a top-three task list. These are the three most important things you need to accomplish. They act as anchors for your day, providing a clear focus and preventing you from getting sidetracked by less important tasks. Review what you've achieved at the end of each week and plan for the week ahead. This routine helps you stay organized and ensures that you're consistently working towards your goals. It's about creating a rhythm that keeps you on track.

Flexibility is crucial when it comes to prioritization. Life is unpredictable, and circumstances can change in the blink of an eye. It's important to reassess your priorities regularly and adjust them as needed. At the end of each day, take a moment to reflect on what you've accomplished and how your priorities might need to shift. This reflection allows you to adapt to new challenges and opportunities, always focusing on what's most important. By remaining flexible, you can navigate the ups and downs of life with greater ease.

Prioritizing tasks without feeling overwhelmed is an ongoing process. It requires practice, patience, and the ability to adapt. However, with tools like the Eisenhower Matrix and focusing on impact, you can create a system that works for you. It's about finding balance, managing your time effectively, and approaching each day with a clear sense of purpose. By honing these skills, you can transform how you approach tasks, reducing stress and increasing productivity. The goal is to empower you to take control of your time and confidently tackle your to-do list.

2.1 Managing Energy Levels for Consistent Cleaning

We've all experienced it: standing in a messy room, full of good intentions but utterly lacking the energy to face the chaos. Energy levels can be as unpredictable as a toddler on a sugar high, yet they play a vital role in our ability to maintain a tidy space. Recognizing when you naturally feel more energetic can change how you approach cleaning. Maybe you're a morning person, ready to tackle the world—or at least the living room—before breakfast. Others might find a burst of energy in the late afternoon or evening. Identifying these peak times is key. It allows you to plan cleaning sessions when you're most likely to be productive, making the task feel less like a chore and more like a natural part of your day.

But what happens when those peak times don't align with your schedule or when life's demands leave you feeling exhausted? That's where energy management comes in. Scheduling breaks and rest periods can keep you from burning out. Think of these breaks as mini-rewards for your efforts, giving you a moment to recharge before diving back in. Incorporating physical activity into your routine can also help. A quick walk around the block or a few jumping jacks can get the blood flowing, providing a natural surge of energy. Physical activity releases endorphins, giving you that extra push needed to tackle cleaning tasks with vigor.

Sometimes, a little boost is all you need to get started. Listening to upbeat music can turn cleaning into a dance party, infusing the task with energy and fun. Choose songs that make you want to move—music has a magical way of lifting spirits and keeping motivation high. I find it difficult to stay motivated if I don't have music when I'm cleaning. Hydration and nutrition also play vital roles in maintaining energy. Dehydration can lead to fatigue, so keep a water bottle nearby and sip regularly. Eating nutrient-rich foods fuels your body to keep going. Think of it as giving your body the right gas for peak performance.

Self-care is another crucial component of energy management. A regular sleep schedule ensures you're well-rested and ready to face the day. Sleep is a powerful restorative tool, and even minor improvements in sleep quality can make a big difference in your energy levels. Mindfulness and relaxation practices, like meditation or deep-breathing exercises, can help you manage stress and maintain a calm, focused mindset. Taking time to unwind and care for yourself isn't just beneficial—it's necessary. These practices refill your energy reserves, helping you approach cleaning with a refreshed perspective.

Incorporating these strategies into your routine isn't about adding more to your to-do list; it's about finding ways to support your natural rhythms and make cleaning a sustainable part of your life. With a bit of planning and a focus on energy management, you can transform those moments of fatigue into opportunities for action. It isn't just about cleaning. It's about creating an environment where you feel energized and at ease, ready to take on whatever life throws your way.

2.2 Tackling Decision Fatigue to Break Through Overwhelm

When you're facing clutter or an endless to-do list, it's not just the task itself that feels overwhelming—it's the sheer number of decisions required to tackle it. Those with ADHD often experience decision fatigue, as the constant need to choose, prioritize, and act drains mental energy. Every item you pick up, every task you assess, demands your attention and requires a decision. Over time, this mental strain can leave you feeling stuck, paralyzed by the inability to make even the simplest choices.

The key to overcoming decision fatigue is simplifying the decision-making process. Start by creating pre-set rules or systems that guide your choices. For instance, adopt a "one-touch rule" for handling clutter: when you pick up an item, decide immediately whether to keep, donate, or toss it. This eliminates the need for prolonged deliberation and keeps you moving forward. Another helpful strategy is to categorize tasks or items before diving in. For example, you can do this by grouping similar objects, such as papers, books, or clothes so that you can make decisions for each category all at once rather than piecemeal.

Limiting the number of decisions you make in a session can also help. Set a timer and commit to making decisions for 10 or 15 minutes. During this time, focus solely on one area, like a drawer or a corner of the room. Knowing there's a time limit reduces the pressure to get everything done and helps you stay focused. If decision-making still feels overwhelming, try starting with the easiest decisions first, like throwing away trash or sorting items you know belong in specific places. Each small decision builds momentum, making it easier to tackle tougher ones.

Finally, give yourself permission to delay non-critical decisions. If you're stuck on something that isn't urgent—like where to store seasonal decorations—set it aside and move on. The goal isn't to make every decision perfectly but to make steady progress. Overcoming decision fatigue is about freeing your mental energy for what matters most and finding confidence in your ability to move forward, one choice at a time.

2.3 Overcoming Perfectionism in Organizing

Imagine standing in front of a cluttered closet, determined to turn it into a pristine, organized haven. Yet, instead of diving in, you hesitate. You might find yourself obsessing over the exact placement of each item, fearing that if it's not perfect, it's not worth doing at all. This is a classic sign of perfectionism, a mindset that often holds us back. Perfectionism can manifest as a reluctance to start tasks, driven by the fear of making mistakes or not meeting self-imposed high standards. You might spend excessive time fixating on minor details, losing sight of the bigger picture. This need for flawlessness can lead to procrastination and overwhelm, and the idea of achieving perfection becomes paralyzing.

> "Done is better than perfect."
>
> Sheryl Sandberg

This simple reminder helps you reframe your goals, encouraging action over hesitation and reminding you that progress, not perfection, is the ultimate aim.

The negative impacts of perfectionism are profound. It can turn what should be a simple organizing task into a source of stress and anxiety.

Instead of feeling accomplished, you may feel stuck and unable to move forward. Pursuing perfection often leads to a cycle of delay as you wait for the "right" moment to start. This can result in clutter accumulating, making the task even more daunting. Understanding these impacts is crucial, as it highlights the need to shift our approach and embrace imperfection as part of the process.

One way to combat perfectionism is by setting realistic goals. This means defining what "good enough" looks like and aiming for that instead of an unattainable ideal. Start by breaking your organizing tasks into smaller, achievable steps. For instance, focus on one shelf or section at a time rather than overhauling your entire closet in one go. This approach reduces the pressure and allows you to experience a sense of progress. Embracing the concept of "good enough" means recognizing that organization is not about achieving a flawless outcome but creating a functional and comfortable space that works for you.

A mindset shift towards progress over perfection can be transformative. Celebrating incremental improvements can foster a sense of accomplishment without needing everything to be perfect. Each small step forward is a victory worth acknowledging. Practicing self-compassion is also crucial. It involves treating yourself with kindness and understanding that mistakes are part of learning. When you let go of perfectionism, you open yourself up to growth and creativity. This shift lets you focus on what truly matters: making your space work for you.

As you navigate the path away from perfectionism, remember that the goal is to create an environment that supports your life, not one that demands constant upkeep and scrutiny. By valuing progress, you ensure that your organizing efforts are sustainable and enjoyable. This perspective makes the process more manageable and helps you build resilience, allowing you to adapt and thrive in your space.

With the insights and strategies explored in this chapter, you're well-equipped to tackle organizing with a fresh perspective. As you continue your journey, remember that perfection is not the goal—progress is. Next, we'll explore creating sustainable habits that align with your unique needs, transforming your space in ways that genuinely resonate with your lifestyle.

Chapter 3

Emotional and Mental Well-Being

Do you ever walk into a room and feel like the clutter around you reflects the chaos in your mind? For those with ADHD, clutter can feel like more than misplaced objects—it's a tangible source of stress and frustration, amplifying anxiety and making even small tasks feel monumental. Addressing clutter isn't just about tidying up; it's about reclaiming peace and creating an environment that supports emotional balance.

Clutter's Impact on Emotional Health

Disorganized spaces can intensify feelings of overwhelm and stress, often mirroring the mental clutter many experience. Studies show that cluttered environments affect focus and decision-making, contributing to feelings of being stuck or incapable of moving forward. Decision fatigue, the mental exhaustion caused by constant choices, exacerbates these challenges, making even basic tasks feel insurmountable. Recognizing this connection between physical and mental clutter is a critical first step toward meaningful change.

Reducing Clutter: Start Small

Tackling clutter doesn't have to be daunting. Begin with a single drawer, a corner of a room, or a storage bin. Small wins build momentum, creating a sense of accomplishment that encourages you to keep going. Designate clutter-free zones in your home where you can retreat for relaxation and focus. These spaces act as sanctuaries, offering a break from the chaos and helping you recharge.

Mindfulness in Decluttering

Approaching decluttering with mindfulness can transform the process. Pause before starting to take a few deep breaths, centering your thoughts. Visualize the relief of a clean space and focus on one task at a time. As you declutter, notice the changes in your surroundings and your mood—these small moments of clarity and calm can be deeply motivating.

Interactive Element: Decluttering Mindfulness Exercise

- Sit quietly for a moment and focus on your breath.
- Visualize the clutter as a weight lifting with each exhale.
- Start with a small task, staying present and aware of how your space and emotions shift as you work.

Remember, the goal isn't perfection. It's about creating a home that nurtures your well-being—a space where you can thrive without the weight of clutter holding you back.

3.1 Mindfulness Practices for Focused Cleaning

Cleaning is often seen as a chore to rush through, but with mindfulness, it can become a calming, grounding activity. Staying present allows you to ease anxiety and bring clarity to your actions.

Focus on the sensory details of each task:

- The rhythmic swish of a mop.
- The warmth of water as you wash dishes.
- The transformation of a clean surface.

Pair this with deep, steady breaths to reduce stress and maintain focus. This approach shifts cleaning from a burdensome task to an opportunity for reflection and care.

Create a calming environment to enhance your mindfulness:

- Play soothing music.
- Use scented candles or essential oils.
- Choose a quiet time to clean without distractions.

Over time, mindful cleaning fosters a sense of balance and fulfillment, turning routine chores into meaningful practices that leave both your space and mind refreshed.

3.2 Managing Anxiety During Organizing Efforts

Organizing can trigger anxiety, especially when the scope feels overwhelming. Fear of not completing tasks or encountering forgotten items often leads to avoidance. To break this cycle, start small. Focus on manageable sections, like a single shelf or cupboard, and celebrate each completed step.

Use grounding techniques to stay present:

- Take deep breaths when anxiety rises.
- Feel your feet on the ground and focus on your surroundings.
- Remind yourself that you're safe and capable of moving forward.

Self-compassion is equally important. Acknowledge progress rather than fixating on what's left to do. Give yourself grace, understanding that change takes time and effort. Incorporate calming practices like listening to soothing music, stretching, or visualizing your ideal space to keep stress at bay.

Calming Practices Reflection Section

Take a moment to reflect on what activities calm you. Jot down a few that resonate—maybe a favorite playlist, a short meditation, or a walk in the fresh air. Keep this list handy for when anxiety starts to creep in during organizing. Use these practices as tools to help you stay grounded and focused.

These strategies are about finding what works for you, easing the anxiety accompanying organizing, and making the process more enjoyable. Organizing doesn't have to be a source of stress. With patience and the right tools, it can become a chance to create balance and foster personal growth.

3.3 Letting Go: Tackling Emotional Attachments to Clutter

Have you ever held onto something because it felt too important to part with, even if it didn't serve you anymore? Maybe it's an old concert T-shirt, a stack of birthday cards, or a kitchen gadget you swore you'd use but never did. For many of us, clutter isn't just stuff; it's emotion made tangible. Each item can carry memories, guilt, or even dreams, making the act of letting go feel daunting and deeply personal.

Why We Hold On

Items often represent more than their physical form. That worn-out college sweatshirt? It might remind you of a time when life felt simpler. The blender you bought during your smoothie phase? It carries the promise of healthier habits you never quite established. Letting go can feel like losing a piece of yourself, a connection to your past, or a hope for the future. For those with ADHD, these emotional attachments can be even stronger, as the thought of deciding what stays and what goes becomes overwhelming.

But here's the truth: letting go doesn't erase memories or diminish dreams. It creates space—both physical and emotional—for what truly matters.

Reframing Letting Go

Instead of focusing on what you're losing, shift your mindset to what you're gaining. Releasing items that no longer serve you opens up room for peace and clarity. That space isn't just for things; it's for you—your growth, your goals, and your well-being. A decluttered space reflects a decluttered mind, reducing the constant mental noise and giving you the freedom to focus on what brings you joy.

Here are some strategies to ease the process of letting go:

- **Start Small:** Choose one low-stakes area, like a junk drawer or a pile of old magazines. Success here can build confidence for tackling more emotionally charged items.

- **Ask the Right Questions:** As you sort through your belongings, ask yourself:
    - Does this item add value to my life today?
    - Would I miss this if I didn't have it?
    - Does keeping this align with the version of myself I want to be?

- **Create a Memory Box:** Designate a small box or container for sentimental items you're not ready to part with. This way, you can honor the memory without letting it dominate your space. Be selective—this box is for your most meaningful keepsakes, not everything you've ever owned.

- **Focus on the Future:** Imagine the organized, clutter-free space you're working toward. Picture how it feels to walk into a room that supports your goals and reflects the life you want to live.

The Emotional Release of Letting Go

Letting go can be surprisingly freeing. As you shed the weight of unused or unnecessary items, you may notice a shift in your emotional state. There's something profoundly satisfying about watching a space transform into one that feels lighter, calmer, and more manageable. You might even feel a sense of pride for making decisions that prioritize your well-being.

It's Okay to Ask for Help

If you're struggling to let go, enlist the support of someone you trust. A friend, family member, or even a professional organizer can offer a fresh perspective and help you navigate tough decisions. They can remind you that it's okay to release items that no longer serve a purpose in your life.

Remember, letting go is not about perfection. It's about creating a space that supports the person you are now, not the person you were or hoped to be. As you release the clutter, you're making room for something far more valuable: clarity, freedom, and the possibility of something new.

3.4 Building Confidence Through Small Wins

A single small win can have a ripple effect, boosting confidence and encouraging further progress. Whether it's tidying a drawer or clearing a desk corner, these victories reinforce positive behavior and build momentum.

Set achievable goals to create instant gratification:

- Spend 10 minutes on one task, like organizing a single shelf.

- Take a step back to appreciate your progress and feel motivated to continue.

Celebrate your accomplishments to sustain confidence. Keep a journal of successes, no matter how small. Over time, this record serves as a reminder of your growth and capabilities. Reward yourself with activities you enjoy, like a favorite snack or a relaxing walk, to acknowledge your efforts.

Supportive self-talk also plays a vital role. Affirmations like "Every small step matters" or "I can create a calm space" build resilience and encourage you to tackle challenges with optimism.

These small wins are stepping stones to larger goals, helping you create lasting confidence and habits that transform your space and mindset. Each victory, however minor, reflects your ability to create positive change. With this approach, future challenges feel more manageable, paving the way for continued success and personal growth.

Chapter 4
ADHD-Friendly Time Management

Ever find yourself staring at a to-do list, feeling like you're juggling a dozen tasks and can't catch a break? You're not alone. When you have ADHD, managing time can feel like trying to hold water in your hands—it keeps slipping through your fingers, no matter how hard you try to hold on. There is a constant struggle to stay focused and on track, overwhelmed by distractions and interruptions. That's where the Pomodoro Technique comes in, a method designed to help anchor your attention and make time management less of a Herculean task and more of an achievable goal. Developed by Francesco Cirillo in the late 1980s, the Pomodoro Technique breaks work into manageable intervals, known as "pomodoros," each lasting 25 minutes, followed by a 5-minute break. These structured sessions fit perfectly with the ADHD brain, offering rhythm and clarity in the chaos.

The beauty of the Pomodoro Technique lies in its simplicity. You can prevent burnout and maintain motivation by working in bursts of focus. It's like having a mental reset button, allowing you to tackle tasks without feeling overwhelmed. These intervals encourage you to concentrate fully, knowing a break is just around the corner. For many, this method helps manage time, stay focused, and reduce mental fatigue, creating a sense of accomplishment with each completed session. However, ADHD minds may need some tweaking to make the most of this technique. Shortening work sessions to 10–15 minutes can make them more manageable, especially when maintaining focus is challenging. It's about finding that sweet spot where you're productive yet comfortable.

Breaks are not just pauses but vital components of the Pomodoro Technique. They offer a chance to recharge and regroup, preventing fatigue from setting in. Incorporating physical movement, a quick stretch or a short walk, and practicing mindfulness or relaxation exercises during breaks can also provide a mental reset. Meditation can calm the mind, readying you for the next focused work session. The key is to use these breaks wisely, ensuring they serve their purpose in maintaining productivity.

Implementing the Pomodoro Technique in your daily routine involves a few straightforward steps. First, set up a timer—a physical timer or apps like Focus Booster or Tomato Timer, specifically designed to help track these intervals. Next, choose tasks for each Pomodoro session. Break larger tasks into smaller, more manageable chunks and assign them to different Pomodoros. This way, you can tackle them one at a time without feeling overwhelmed. As you work through each session, focus solely on the task. When the timer signals the end of a Pomodoro, take your break and allow your mind to wander. This balance of focus and relaxation is the core of the technique.

Interactive Element: Customized Pomodoro Planner

Create a Customized Pomodoro Planner to help guide your sessions. Identify three tasks you want to accomplish today. Break each task into smaller parts and assign each part to a Pomodoro session. Use a timer app to track and note how you feel before and after each session. Adjust the length of work sessions and breaks to find what works best. This planner can become a tool to refine your use of the Pomodoro Technique, adapting it to fit your lifestyle and needs.

The Pomodoro Technique can transform how you manage time. It offers a structured yet flexible approach that suits the ebb and flow of life with ADHD. By embracing its principles and customizing them to your needs, you can find a rhythm that works for you, turning time from a foe into a friend.

4.1 Timeboxing: Maximizing Focus and Efficiency

Timeboxing is like your personal productivity guide, a straightforward technique that helps you precisely manage your schedule. By allocating fixed time slots to specific tasks, you create a clear structure for your day. Imagine each task as a puzzle piece, fitting snugly into a designated time block on your daily schedule. This method allows you to focus on one thing at a time, reducing the mental clutter that often accompanies a busy day. It's about building a daily rhythm, where tasks have dedicated moments, allowing you to move through your day purposefully and efficiently. For those with ADHD, this approach is a game-changer, offering clarity and reducing the stress of decision fatigue.

The beauty of timeboxing lies in its structured approach to tackling tasks, making it a powerful tool to combat procrastination. By assigning each task a specific time frame, you eliminate the open-endedness that can lead to constant delays. This framework provides a sense of urgency, encouraging you to start and finish tasks within the allotted time. Knowing your next task has a waiting time slot can motivate you to keep moving forward. It's like having a personal coach gently nudging you to stay on track. When you account for every minute, there's less room for distractions to creep in, helping you maintain focus and momentum throughout the day.

To effectively implement timeboxing, create a schedule that outlines your day in blocks. Use digital calendars or planners to visualize your time, making adjustments as needed. Begin by listing out your tasks and estimating how long each will take. Remember, it's important to be realistic about the time required for each task. Once you've identified these time frames, assign them to specific blocks in your schedule. Adjust the length of your time blocks based on the complexity and importance of the tasks. For example, more straightforward tasks might need shorter time slots, while more involved projects may require more extended periods. Striking a balance between work and personal time is also crucial. Ensure your schedule includes time for breaks and activities that recharge you, preventing burnout.

Timeboxing can be incredibly versatile, fitting into various organizational tasks. Consider organizing a cluttered closet. Instead of tackling the entire project at once, break it down into 30-minute increments. Dedicate each increment to a specific section or type of item, such as shoes or sweaters. This approach makes the task feel more manageable and less overwhelming.

Similarly, timeboxing is helpful for digital decluttering sessions. Schedule short, focused periods to sort through emails or organize digital files. These intermittent sessions prevent digital chaos from building up, keeping your virtual space tidy.

Mastering Timeboxing
Your Guide to Focus and Productivity

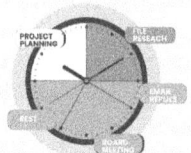

WHAT IS TIMEBOXING?

Timeboxing is a productivity technique where you allocate specific time blocks for tasks, helping you focus and complete them efficiently.

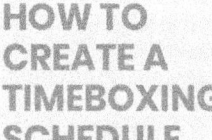

- Reduces procrastination.
- Provides structure to your day.
- Limits time spent on perfectionism.
- Encourages focus by setting clear boundaries.

Step-by-Step Guide:

1. **List Your Tasks:** Write down everything you need to accomplish for the day.
2. **Estimate Time:** Approximate how long each task will take.
3. **Prioritize:** Use a tool like the Eisenhower Matrix to determine urgent and important tasks.
4. **Set Time Blocks:** Assign specific time slots for each task.
   Example: 9:00-9:30 Morning Emails, 9:30-10:30 Deep Work.
5. **Include Breaks:** Add short breaks between time blocks to recharge.
6. **Stick to the Schedule:** Use timers or alarms to signal when it's time to move to the next task.

HOW TO CREATE A TIMEBOXING SCHEDULE

TIMEBOXING TIPS FOR ADHD

- **Start small:** Begin with just one or two time blocks per day to build the habit.
- **Be realistic:** Avoid over-scheduling—leave room for flexibility.
- **Add buffers:** Allow extra time for tasks to prevent rushing.
- **Celebrate wins:** Take a moment to acknowledge completing a time block, no matter how small

THE ADHD CONNECTION

Why It Works for ADHD:
- Prevents hyperfocus on one task at the expense of others.
- Makes large tasks less overwhelming by breaking them into smaller, time-defined chunks.
- Provides a sense of accomplishment after completing each block.
- Combats the tendency to lose track of time.

TOOLS TO HELP WITH TIMEBOXING

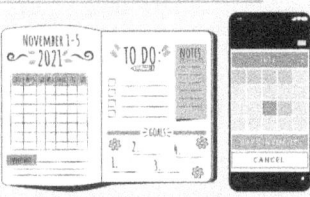

Digital Tools:
- Google Calendar (Set color-coded time blocks).
- Trello or Notion (Visualize your schedule and track tasks).
- Pomodoro Timer Apps (Combine focus sprints with breaks).

Physical Tools:
- A planner or journal with pre-designed time-blocking sections.
- A kitchen timer or alarm clock to signal transitions.

TOOLS TO HELP WITH TIMEBOXING

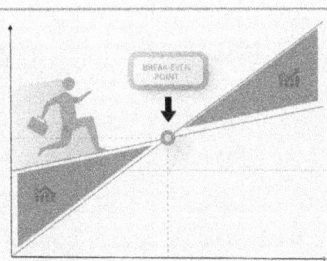

CHALLENGES
- Underestimating time needed for tasks.
- Getting distracted during a block.
- Feeling overwhelmed by rigid schedules.

SOLUTIONS
- Use a timer to stay on track.
- Adjust your time blocks as needed—timeboxing is flexible!
- Remember, it's okay if you don't finish every task; reschedule as needed.

TIMEBOXING IS YOUR ROADMAP TO PRODUCTIVITY—ONE BLOCK AT A TIME!
With timeboxing, even the busiest days can feel manageable. Give it a try and see how structure creates freedom.

Visual Element: Timeboxing Scheduler Template

Consider creating a Timeboxing Scheduler Template to help organize your tasks. Design a simple table with columns for the task, duration, and time slot. Fill in your tasks and estimated durations, and assign them to specific time slots throughout your day. Visualizing your schedule this way can provide clarity and help maintain focus, ensuring that each task gets the attention it deserves.

Timeboxing offers a structured yet flexible way to navigate your day, helping you make the most of each moment. By embracing this method, you can create a more organized and efficient routine, turning time from a source of stress into a tool for success.

4.2 Task Stacking: Grouping Tasks for Better Flow

Ever felt like you're constantly switching gears, jumping from one task to another without really getting into the flow? That's where task stacking comes in—a simple yet effective strategy to streamline your workflow by grouping similar tasks. Imagine tackling all your email replies in one go instead of spacing them awkwardly throughout the day. By grouping tasks that require similar mindsets or tools, you save precious mental energy and reduce the fatigue from constant task-switching.

For those with ADHD, task stacking can be a lifesaver. It helps maintain focus by creating a rhythm and reducing the chaos of jumping between unrelated tasks. When your brain doesn't have to shift gears constantly, you can achieve a deeper level of focus, making you more efficient. Think of it as assembling ingredients before cooking a meal—when everything is prepped, and in its place, the process flows smoothly and efficiently. Plus, it minimizes the risk of distractions because you're less likely to change direction needlessly. This can help make your day feel less scattered and more intentional.

Identifying stackable tasks might initially seem daunting, but it's easier than it sounds. Start by looking at your daily routine and pinpointing tasks that naturally go together. Administrative tasks like paying bills or scheduling are often most efficiently managed when grouped in a single dedicated block of time. Similarly, home maintenance chores, such as dusting and vacuuming, can be grouped into a single cleaning session. Grouping tasks simplifies your schedule, allowing you to approach your day with clarity and focus, knowing exactly what you need to do and when.

Take a closer look at how task stacking can transform routines. Consider your morning routine: Instead of getting sidetracked by emails or social media, dedicate that time to activities like showering, dressing, and preparing breakfast. This creates a smooth and efficient transition into your day, minimizing distractions and setting a positive tone. An evening wind-down stack could include tidying up, setting up for the next day, and reading before bed. Stacking these tasks creates a consistent routine requiring less mental effort.

Task stacking doesn't just make life easier; it adds a sense of accomplishment. Each completed stack is a mini-victory, reinforcing your ability to stay organized and efficient. As you get better at recognizing and creating stacks, you'll find your day running more smoothly, with fewer interruptions and more time for what truly matters. The key is to stay flexible, adapting your stacks to fit changing priorities and demands.

4.3 Managing Squirrel Moments: Staying on Track

"Squirrel moments" happen when you're intensely focused on a task but suddenly get distracted by something entirely unrelated. With ADHD, these moments are all too familiar. A sudden noise, a stray thought, or even the sight of something out of place can pull your attention away, making it difficult to return to the original task. These episodes of distraction are like little detours that can derail your productivity, turning what should be a simple task into a prolonged struggle. The challenge lies in managing these distractions and finding a way back to focus once the moment has passed.

Creating a distraction-free workspace is an essential part of minimizing these interruptions. Start by setting up an area free from clutter and unnecessary items. A clean, organized space can help keep your mind on track. Consider using focus-enhancing tools and apps to maintain concentration. Apps that block distracting websites, like Cold Turkey or Freedom, can keep your attention where it needs to be. Silencing or turning off notifications on your devices is another effective strategy. Without the constant pinging of alerts, your mind can settle into a task without the temptation to check messages or emails.

But what happens when, despite your best efforts, you find yourself pulled away by a "squirrel moment"? Regaining focus after an interruption is key. Practicing mindfulness techniques can assist in bringing your attention back to the task at hand. Try taking a few deep breaths, focusing on the present moment, and gently redirecting your thoughts. Implementing brief structured breaks can also help. These mini-pauses allow your brain to reset, reducing the frustration of diving back into work after a distraction. Setting boundaries with family or roommates can provide you the space to concentrate. Let others know when you need uninterrupted time, creating an environment that supports your focus.

Beyond managing distractions, keeping tasks engaging can prevent your mind from wandering. One way to do this is by turning mundane tasks into a time race. Set a timer and see how much you can accomplish before it goes off, adding a playful element to your work. Breaking tasks into smaller, engaging challenges can also make them more captivating. By focusing on completing one small part at a time, you create a series of achievable goals, each offering its own reward. This approach maintains interest and builds momentum, carrying you through to the task's completion.

Interactive Element: Distraction-Proof Your Space Checklist

Take a moment to evaluate your workspace. Is there clutter? Are there devices that need silencing? Create a checklist of steps to make your space distraction-proof. Consider adding focus-enhancing tools or apps to your routine. Once your space is ready, notice how these changes impact your ability to focus and complete tasks. This checklist is a simple yet powerful tool to help create an environment conducive to productivity.

With these strategies, you can transform "squirrel moments" from stumbling blocks into opportunities to hone your focus.

4.4 Handling Deadlines and Time Constraints with Ease

Deadlines. Even hearing the word can feel overwhelming, especially when you're living with ADHD. They can loom large, casting shadows of anxiety and pressure, often making productivity feel like an uphill battle. Deadlines demand attention and prioritize themselves in your mind, creating a sense of urgency that can motivate and paralyze. For many, the ticking clock heightens stress, sparking a rush of adrenaline that may lead to scattered focus rather than efficient action. It's as if the closer the deadline, the harder it becomes to concentrate, and the easier it is to fall into the trap of procrastination.

Effectively managing these deadlines requires a strategic approach. Start by breaking down each deadline into smaller, manageable milestones. Think of it as slicing a pie into pieces rather than trying to eat it whole. Setting personal deadlines ahead of the actual ones gives you a buffer zone. This strategy reduces anxiety and allows room for adjustments without the last-minute panic. Each milestone becomes a mini-deadline, helping you progress steadily and reducing the overwhelming nature of the final due date.

In the age of technology, digital tools and apps can be lifesavers for keeping track of deadlines. Calendar reminders are simple yet powerful tools for ensuring deadlines don't sneak up on you. Set reminders a few days in advance to give yourself ample preparation time. Project management apps like Trello or Asana can also help. They allow you to organize tasks, set deadlines, and visualize your progress. These tools offer a centralized space to track everything, preventing important tasks from slipping through the cracks. With notifications and visual timelines, staying on top of deadlines becomes less of a daunting challenge and more of a manageable routine.

When deadlines approach, maintain composure while navigating the pressure. The breathing exercises we touched on earlier can be your secret weapon. Take a moment to inhale deeply, hold, and exhale slowly. This practice calms the nervous system, reducing stress and increasing focus. Prioritizing tasks based on urgency and importance can also help. Use a simple matrix to distinguish between what needs immediate attention and what can wait. This clarity allows you to focus your energy on high-impact tasks, ensuring you're working on what truly matters.

Stress-relief techniques, like mindfulness or short walks, can provide a much-needed break from the intensity of deadlines. Taking a 5-minute pause to clear your mind can rejuvenate your focus, providing a fresh perspective when you return to work. This approach enhances productivity and promotes well-being, ensuring burnout won't happen by the end of the deadline rush.

As you become adept at handling deadlines, the pressure will lessen, allowing you to navigate time constraints with confidence. With these strategies, deadlines transform from intimidating to manageable, empowering you to tackle them head-on.

By mastering these time management techniques, you'll develop a toolkit that extends beyond work and enhances your daily life. Next, we'll explore how to build sustainable habits that align with your unique needs, crafting routines that support both productivity and peace.

Chapter 5

Building Sustainable Habits

Have you ever noticed how some days it feels like your entire routine is in perfect harmony, each task flowing seamlessly into the next, like the notes of your favorite song? Yet, other days, it's as if the melody is lost, and you're left scrambling to keep up with the chaos. The key to finding that rhythm lies in building sustainable habits—a challenge for anyone, but especially when you struggle with ADHD. These habits are like the sheet music of our daily lives, guiding our actions and helping us navigate the complexities of each day with confidence and ease.

Enter the world of habit stacking, a concept that can transform how you approach routines. Habit stacking involves linking a new habit to an existing one, creating a chain reaction that makes both habits stick. Here's how it works:

- **Anchor a new habit to an existing one:** Use routines you already follow as triggers for new behaviors.

- **Start small:** Choose habits that require minimal effort to build momentum.

- **Keep it consistent:** Perform the habits together regularly until they become second nature.

For example, pairing your morning coffee with a quick 5-minute tidy-up of your workspace creates an effortless flow. Similarly, setting out clothes for the next day before bed simplifies your mornings and reduces decision-making.

Habit stacking reduces the cognitive load often associated with starting new routines, making it an ideal strategy for those with ADHD. The existing habit acts as a trigger, prompting the new behavior and simplifying the process. This approach reduces the mental energy required to initiate tasks, freeing you to focus on other priorities. It's like having a trusted guide that leads you through your day, allowing you to build consistency without feeling overwhelmed. The beauty of habit stacking lies in its simplicity, transforming the daunting process of creating new habits into something manageable and enjoyable.

To identify stackable habits:

- Start by analyzing your daily routine and pinpointing existing behaviors.

- Look for natural pairings and activities that fit seamlessly without disrupting your flow.

- For instance, consider a quick room scan after brushing your teeth to find misplaced items. This small addition can help maintain a tidy space without feeling like an extra chore.

The goal is to find habits that complement each other, creating a harmonious routine that supports your lifestyle. It's about enhancing your current habits rather than overhauling your entire routine.

Examples of successful habit stacks illustrate how combining tasks can lead to stronger routines. Consider pairing breakfast with a quick review of your daily schedule. While enjoying your meal, glance over your planner or calendar, giving you a clear picture of the day ahead. This habit stack grounds you in the present moment and prepares you for future tasks. By anchoring new behaviors to established routines, habit stacking makes incorporating positive changes into your daily life easier.

Interactive Element: Habit Stacking Worksheet

Take a moment to create your habit-stacking worksheet. List your current daily habits, then identify new habits you'd like to incorporate. Find natural pairings and write them down, noting how they fit into your existing routine. Use this worksheet to track your progress and adjust as needed, ensuring your habit stacks support your goals and lifestyle. This tool is a tangible reminder of your commitment to building sustainable habits, providing a roadmap to guide your journey.

5.1 Turning Routines into Rituals for Consistency

Routines and rituals may seem similar, but they serve distinct purposes in our daily lives. Routines provide the structured framework for tasks we perform regularly, bringing order and predictability. Rituals, however, go beyond structure by adding intention and meaning, transforming everyday actions into moments of mindfulness.

For example:

- A morning routine might include savoring a calming cup of tea paired with a moment of reflection to set a positive tone for the day.

- Lighting a scented candle before cleaning can create a sensory signal, marking the start of focused effort.

- Playing a favorite song at the beginning of a work session can mentally prepare you for productivity.

Rituals elevate the mundane, grounding us amidst life's chaos. For individuals with ADHD, this sense of stability can be particularly helpful, offering a reassuring anchor when unpredictability looms.

The psychological benefits of rituals are significant. They provide familiarity and comfort, creating a steady framework to stabilize the mind, sharpen focus, and reduce anxiety. Turning routines into rituals invites mindfulness into your day, shifting the goal from simply completing tasks to truly engaging in them.

The beauty of rituals lies in their simplicity; small adjustments can bring significant impact. Replacing evening screen time with a good book can relax the mind and establish a nightly ritual signaling the end of the day. These thoughtful habits foster consistency and create moments to reconnect with yourself. Rituals can be as simple as expressing gratitude before sleep or setting a daily intention with your morning coffee. The key is to choose actions that resonate with your values and bring calm, creating a rhythm that supports your life.

Incorporating rituals into your routines enriches daily life, turning repetitive tasks into opportunities for reflection and joy. Reflect on small actions that bring you peace or happiness, and explore how to weave them into your existing habits. By adding intention to your routines, you can create a life that feels organized, meaningful, and aligned with your personal priorities.

5.2 The Power of Visual Reminders in Habit Building

Imagine walking around your home and seeing small, colorful cues guiding you through your day—sticky notes on doors reminding you of tasks or a vibrant calendar in your kitchen mapping out your week. For those with ADHD, visual reminders can be lifesavers, providing the nudges needed to stay on track. They help anchor your thoughts and keep your focus aligned with your goals. The brain processes visuals faster and more effectively than words, making these cues particularly effective. A sticky note with a simple "Don't forget lunch!" on the fridge or a bright reminder on your mirror each morning can make a world of difference.

Visual reminders don't have to be bland or uninspired. They can be as creative as you are! Consider color-coded calendars for task management, where each color represents a different category or level of urgency. This makes it easy to prioritize and adds a splash of color to your day. Vision boards are another fantastic option, especially for long-term goals. Filled with inspiring images and words, they serve as constant motivators, keeping your aspirations front and center. Whether it's a picture of a dream destination or quotes that uplift you, these boards can transform your space into a haven of inspiration.

Customizing visual aids to fit your personality and environment can make them even more effective. Personalized to-do lists with visual icons can help transform your tasks from mundane to engaging. For instance, using a sun icon for morning tasks or a moon for nighttime chores can add a touch of fun and clarity. The key is to make these aids not just functional but also enjoyable to use. By aligning them with your tastes, you create a system that feels less like a chore and more like a support network tailored just for you.

Keeping spaces orderly while using visual cues requires a bit of strategy. It's easy for these reminders to become just another part of the clutter if not managed well. Rotating reminders is a smart tactic to avoid desensitization—change them up regularly to keep them fresh and eye-catching. Digital tools can also be beneficial here. Reminder apps on your phone or tablet serve as portable visual cues to ensure you have nudges throughout the day without adding to your physical clutter. Whether it's a pop-up notification or a gentle vibration, digital reminders can be discreet yet effective.

How Visual Aids Empower ADHD Minds

Visual tools transform abstract ideas into clear, actionable steps, making organization easier and more intuitive for ADHD brains.

Calendars
See Your Time Clearly

TIPS

Use **color-coded time blocks:** Assign colors to categories (e.g., green for personal, blue for work).

Opt for **monthly, weekly, and daily views** to balance long-term and immediate planning.

KEY BENEFITS

- Provides structure to your day.
- Reduces decision fatigue by laying out tasks in advance.
- Helps you stay aware of deadlines.

Habit Trackers
Build Momentum, One Step at a Time

TIPS

Keep it fun and visual—use stickers or colors to track progress.

Pair habits with a goal (e.g., complete 7 days = reward).

ORGANIZING & CLEANING WITH ADHD

KEY BENEFITS

- Provides instant feedback on progress.
- Encourages consistency and accountability.
- Turns habit-building into a rewarding experience.

TYPES OF HABIT TRACKERS

- **Daily Progress Bars:** Fill in as you complete tasks (e.g., drink water, tidy up).
- **Weekly Checklists:** Simple boxes to tick off tasks (e.g., clean workspace, plan meals).
- **Streak Trackers:** Visualize how many consecutive days you've completed a habit.

To-Do Lists and Task Prioritization
Turn Overwhelm into Order

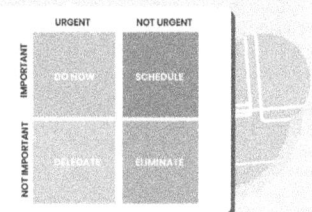

TIPS

Keep it visible
(on a wall, desk, or app).

Include deadlines and
time estimates for each task.

KEY BENEFITS

- Breaks down large tasks into smaller, manageable steps.
- Keeps focus on high-priority tasks while leaving room for flexibility.

TYPES OF HABIT TRACKERS

- **Use the Eisenhower Matrix:** Categorize tasks by urgent/important, important/not urgent, etc.
- Color-coded or segmented to-do lists (e.g., today's tasks vs. long-term tasks).
- Highlight three top priorities for the day to reduce decision fatigue.

Find What Works for You!

Whether it's a colorful calendar, a motivational habit tracker, or a dynamic to-do list, visual tools are your secret weapon for clarity and focus.

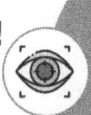

Start with one tool today and watch how visual organization transforms your routines

Visual Element: Create Your Visual Cue Board

Take a piece of poster board and create your visual cue board. Use colorful markers, stickers, or magazine cutouts to outline your weekly tasks or goals. Consider adding inspirational quotes or images that resonate with you. Hang it in a place you'll see daily, like your home office or kitchen. This board will serve as a vibrant reminder of your goals and add a personal touch to your space.

Visual reminders are powerful allies in the quest for organization, transforming abstract intentions into tangible actions. They bring clarity to the chaos, helping you navigate your day with purpose and focus. As you integrate these tools into your life, you'll find them invaluable in keeping distractions at bay and maintaining the momentum toward your goals.

5.3 Maintaining Motivation Through Habit Challenges

Keeping motivation alive over time can feel like a roller coaster, especially when building new habits. One way to keep the excitement going is by setting short-term goals. These goals act like checkpoints, helping you track progress and giving you something to aim for in the near future. When you hit these milestones, take the time to celebrate with small rewards. It could be as simple as treating yourself to a favorite snack or a quiet evening with a good book or your favorite series on Netflix. These little celebrations reinforce your achievements and make the process of building habits much more enjoyable.

Turning habits into games is another fantastic way to make the process more appealing. Gamifying habit formation adds a layer of fun, transforming what might feel like a chore into an engaging activity. Think of it as turning your daily routine into a quest. You could set challenges like daily gratitude journaling for a month. Each day, you jot down something you're thankful for, and at the end of the month, you can look back at all the positive moments. This not only builds a habit but also boosts your mood and outlook.

Finding ways to reignite the spark is crucial when motivation starts to dip—and it inevitably will. Consider rotating organizing tasks to maintain variety. Switching things up prevents monotony and keeps your interest alive. Another strategy is to revisit the initial reasons you started these habits. Reflecting on your "why" can renew your commitment and remind you of the benefits you're working toward. It's like refreshing the page, giving you a new perspective and energy to continue.

Tracking your progress is essential for staying motivated. Habit-tracking apps like Habitica or Streaks can be incredibly helpful. They visually represent your progress, showing you how far you've come and what you've achieved. Physical progress charts are another option. They offer a tangible way to mark your journey, giving you a sense of accomplishment each time you fill a box or move a marker. These tools constantly remind you of your growth, encouraging you to keep going even on challenging days.

Additionally, engaging with external resources can bolster your motivation. Joining online communities focused on ADHD and organization connects you with others who understand your experiences. These communities offer support, advice, and camaraderie. Sharing your successes and struggles with like-minded individuals can be incredibly motivating. It's a reminder that you're not alone, and a network of people are cheering you on. We'll touch more on this in Chapter 10.

Maintaining motivation through habit challenges requires creativity and a willingness to adapt. It's about finding what keeps you engaged and excited, turning the process into something that feels less like work and more like a rewarding adventure. By embracing these strategies, you can create a habit-building experience that's not only effective but also enjoyable.

5.4 Dealing with Setbacks: Resilience in Routine

Setbacks are a natural part of building habits, especially when ADHD is part of the equation. Life is unpredictable, and sometimes, despite our best intentions, routines get disrupted, but when they occur:

- **Identify the cause**: Reflect on whether stress, scheduling conflicts, or low energy were factors.

- **Adjust your approach**: Modify your routines to fit current circumstances without abandoning your goals.

- **Practice self-compassion**: Acknowledge progress instead of fixating on mistakes.

It's important to remember that everyone experiences setbacks and bumps in the road, but these don't define our journey. Accepting that setbacks will happen can ease the pressure we often put on ourselves to be perfect.

When a setback occurs, the first step is to understand why it happened. Analyzing the cause helps prevent it from happening again. This reflection isn't about assigning blame but understanding the factors at play. Once you've identified the root cause, adjust your expectations and goals. Life changes, and so should your plans. This flexibility allows you to tailor your routines to fit your current circumstances, making them more sustainable.

Cultivating a resilient mindset is the key to overcoming setbacks. View these moments as learning opportunities rather than roadblocks. Focus on progress instead of perfection. Celebrate what you've accomplished, and let that drive you forward. Practicing self-compassion during these times is crucial. Be patient with yourself as you navigate the ups and downs of habit-building. It's okay to stumble—what matters is getting back up and moving forward.

For the longest time, I struggled to exercise consistently, especially with little kids, and life felt like a whirlwind. I started with 10 or 15 minutes of short workouts to ease back into the habit without overwhelming myself. Slowly, those short sessions became longer as I found my rhythm again. If I missed my usual workout time, I prioritized fitting it in later in the day, even if it meant getting creative with my schedule. It wasn't always perfect, but because it mattered to me, I learned to be flexible and keep showing up. This adaptive approach allowed me to find a rhythm that worked, proving that resilience and flexibility can lead to success.

When a good friend was assigned to reorganize an entire department at his company, he wasn't even sure where to start. New to the role and without any prior experience in department management, he was taking on a massive responsibility—and he was doing it with ADHD. Instead of letting it overwhelm him, he turned his natural strengths into superpowers. His ADHD made him fast-paced and detail-oriented, able to see the big picture and the small inefficiencies others missed. He devised a system for the team that brought clarity, improved workflows, and fostered a stronger team bond.

By the end of the project, his confidence had skyrocketed. He didn't just feel proud; he knew he'd made a lasting impact. His ability to bring order to a department, something he never imagined possible, showed him that ADHD could be more than a challenge—it could be a unique advantage. These examples highlight the power of resilience and the importance of adapting strategies to fit individual needs.

As you encounter setbacks, remember that they're part of the process. Each challenge is an opportunity to refine your approach and strengthen your resolve. By embracing resilience, you build habits that endure, even in the face of adversity. Setbacks are not the end; they're simply a part of the journey toward creating routines that enhance your life.

Chapter 6

Breaking Down Tasks into Manageable Steps

Have you ever found yourself staring at a to-do list so long it feels like you need a map to navigate it? Those endless tasks can become a cloud, casting shadows over your day. You might feel like you're drowning in a sea of chores, unsure where to begin. It's not uncommon for tasks to seem both overwhelming and impossible. The key to taming this chaos lies in breaking tasks down into manageable steps, and that's where the 5-Minute Task Technique comes into play. This simple yet powerful method can transform your productivity approach, helping you easily conquer that daunting list.

The 5-Minute Task Technique simplifies productivity by breaking tasks into manageable five-minute increments. This approach prevents overwhelm by transforming daunting projects into a series of small, achievable steps. Instead of feeling paralyzed by the size of the task, you can focus on short, focused efforts that maintain momentum and prevent fatigue. By encouraging immediate action, this method helps you overcome procrastination and tackle those dreaded to-dos.

It's also an effective way to make use of small pockets of time that might otherwise be wasted. These brief intervals become opportunities for progress, allowing you to chip away at larger projects without feeling burdened. By breaking tasks into bite-sized chunks, you create a steady rhythm of productivity that feels both achievable and rewarding.

To incorporate the 5-Minute Task Technique into your daily routine, identify tasks that lend themselves to this approach. Look for activities that can be broken down into smaller parts, whether sorting a stack of mail, organizing a drawer, or doing a quick kitchen clean-up. Once you've identified these tasks, set a timer for five minutes. The timer creates a sense of urgency, motivating you to start and complete the task within the allotted time. It's like a race against the clock but in a fun way. This method makes tasks feel more achievable and instills a sense of accomplishment as you check each one off your list.

This technique shines in numerous scenarios. Imagine tackling a messy desk by committing to just five minutes of sorting paperwork.

You'd be surprised at how much you can accomplish in such a short time. Or consider the impact of dedicating five minutes to tidying up your kitchen, clearing counters, and putting away dishes. These small efforts can make a significant difference, creating a more organized and inviting space. The beauty of this technique is its flexibility—it can be applied to various tasks, allowing you to adjust your approach based on your needs and energy levels.

The psychological benefits of quick wins are profound. Completing small tasks boosts motivation and confidence, reinforcing your ability to manage your responsibilities. No matter how small, each victory reduces anxiety about more significant projects, making them feel less daunting. It's like building a ladder from small successes that help you reach greater heights. This method empowers you to take control of your day, one five-minute interval at a time, transforming how you approach tasks and enhancing your overall productivity.

Interactive Element: Quick Win Task List

Create your own Quick Win Task List by jotting down tasks you could complete in five minutes or less. Include activities like sorting a drawer, wiping a countertop, or responding to a quick email. Use this list to fill in those awkward time gaps throughout your day, turning moments of downtime into opportunities for productivity. As you complete each task, check it off and savor the sense of accomplishment that comes with these small victories. This list is a tangible reminder of your progress and potential, motivating you to continue breaking down larger tasks into manageable steps.

6.1 Micro-Cleaning Sessions: Achieving More with Less

Imagine your home as a living, breathing entity that thrives when given consistent, gentle care rather than sporadic, intense attention. This is the essence of micro-cleaning sessions, designed to maintain a tidy environment through brief, targeted cleaning bursts. These sessions focus on high-impact areas, the spots in our homes that quickly become cluttered but can transform with just a little TLC. Think of it as tending to a garden; a little weeding keeps it blooming beautifully without needing an overhaul. Quick tasks like wiping down frequently used surfaces or organizing a cluttered entryway bring immediate results, creating a sense of order beyond the physical space.

To set up effective micro-cleaning sessions, prioritize areas based on need and frequency. Kitchens and living rooms often benefit from daily attention due to their constant use. Bedrooms and bathrooms might follow a slightly less frequent schedule, yet they still deserve regular upkeep. Use a checklist to track progress and help you stay organized while providing a visual reminder of your accomplishments. Imagine walking through your home with this checklist, ticking off each task as you go. A checklist offers structure, ensuring you haven't missed anything while allowing flexibility to adjust priorities as needed.

The benefits of regular micro-cleaning are numerous. First, it helps maintain a baseline of cleanliness, preventing clutter from ever reaching overwhelming levels. It's like setting your home to autopilot, where a consistent effort results in a tidy space. Keeping messes manageable reduces the need for extensive cleaning sessions that can feel daunting and time-consuming. Instead of dedicating an entire day to scrubbing and organizing, these small efforts accumulate, leaving you with more spare time and less stress. The beauty of this approach lies in its simplicity; it's about doing a little each day to achieve a lot over time.

Integrating micro-cleaning into daily life is easier than you might think. Pair cleaning tasks with existing daily activities to make them feel natural. For example, take a minute to wipe down the bathroom sink or straighten up the countertop while brushing your teeth. This pairing turns cleaning into a seamless part of your routine, making it feel less like a chore and more like a habit. Set reminders to prompt cleaning sessions at times that make sense for you, like right before dinner or after your morning coffee. These gentle nudges help establish a rhythm, creating a natural flow that incorporates cleaning into your day without disruption.

Interactive Element: Micro-Cleaning Checklist

Consider creating a Micro-Cleaning Checklist tailored to your home's needs. To get started, scan the QR code at the beginning of this book to access a free printable cleaning checklist and other helpful resources. List high-impact areas that require regular attention and assign specific tasks for each. Include simple actions like clearing the entryway, tidying the living room, or wiping down the kitchen counters. Use this checklist as a guide to direct your micro-cleaning sessions, ensuring every area receives consistent care.

This tool helps keep your space tidy and reminds you of the power of small, consistent efforts in maintaining a clean and inviting home. Remember, the goal of micro-cleaning is not perfection but progress. It's about finding balance and creating an environment where you can thrive without the burden of clutter. By embracing these brief sessions, you'll find that achieving a tidy home is possible and enjoyable. With each small action, you contribute to a larger picture of order and peace within your living space.

6.2 Task Stacking for Maximum Efficiency

Picture this: your day is a series of scattered tasks, each pulling you in a different direction. It's like trying to juggle while riding a unicycle. For anyone with ADHD, this scenario feels all too familiar. That's where task stacking comes in, a method designed to bring order to the chaos by grouping similar tasks. It's about creating a logical flow in your day, minimizing disruptions, and maximizing productivity. Stacking tasks reduces the mental gymnastics required to switch between unrelated activities, allowing you to focus your energy more effectively. Think of it as organizing your day into a seamless sequence, where each task naturally leads into the next, reducing the cognitive load of constant transitions.

To effectively implement task stacking, identify tasks with common elements. For instance, you can group tasks by location, such as completing all kitchen-related chores in one session, or by tools needed, like using the same cleaning products for multiple surfaces. Scheduling similar tasks consecutively helps maintain momentum, as your brain doesn't have to adjust to a new context. It's like creating a playlist of your favorite songs—everything flows once you're in the groove. This approach increases efficiency and makes your day feel more cohesive, reducing the stress of jumping from one task to another.

Imagine meal prepping followed immediately by kitchen cleaning. You're already in the kitchen with ingredients and utensils, so tidying up right after preparing meals makes sense. This stack eliminates the need to return later, saving time and effort. Another scenario might involve laundry sorting and folding. Once you've started sorting clothes, it's natural to continue folding and putting them away. This sequence keeps you in the laundry mindset, allowing you to finish the task without unnecessary breaks. By stacking these related activities, you create a rhythm that streamlines your efforts, transforming mundane chores into manageable tasks.

The benefits of task stacking extend beyond just saving time. This method simplifies organizing efforts by reducing the mental clutter associated with task-switching. When your brain isn't constantly adjusting to new contexts, you can focus more intensely on each task, improving speed and quality. Additionally, task stacking fosters a sense of accomplishment. As you move through each group of activities, you gain momentum, building confidence with each completed stack. This positive reinforcement can boost motivation, making tackling even the most daunting to-do lists easier. Task stacking also provides a framework for planning your day, helping you see where tasks fit in relation to each other and ensuring you make efficient use of your time.

As you explore task stacking, remember to be flexible. While having a plan is important, life is unpredictable, and adapting to changes is equally crucial. Be open to adjusting your stacks, whether shifting tasks around or re-evaluating priorities. With practice, task stacking can become a valuable tool in your organizational toolkit, helping you navigate your day with confidence and ease.

6.3 Overcoming Procrastination with Brain Dumps

Imagine your mind as a crowded room filled with buzzing thoughts bouncing off the walls, each vying for your attention. This mental clutter can become overwhelming, especially when you're trying to focus on organizing your tasks. Enter the brain dump—a technique that helps clear this mental chaos by transferring those thoughts onto paper.

It's about unloading everything without judgment or structure to reduce mental overload and anxiety. Doing this creates space for clarity and focus, allowing you to see what truly needs attention. For many with ADHD, whose minds race with ideas and reminders, brain dumping offers relief, a way to quiet the noise and make sense of the whirlwind within.

To perform a successful brain dump, it's crucial to set aside dedicated time for this process. Think of it as a mental declutter session, where you aim to empty your mind onto a page. Find a quiet space, free from distractions, and equip yourself with the tools you prefer—whether that's a trusty notebook or a digital app. The key is to let your thoughts flow freely, writing down everything that comes to mind. Don't worry about organization at this stage; the goal is to transfer your mental load onto something tangible. Externalizing your thoughts can provide immediate relief as if you've lifted a weight off your shoulders.

After finishing your brain dump, the next step is transforming the chaos into actionable tasks. This is the moment where clarity emerges as you sort through the clutter to pinpoint what truly matters. Look for patterns or common themes and start categorizing your thoughts. Which tasks are urgent? Which can wait? By sorting your ideas into manageable categories, you create a roadmap for action, turning what was once overwhelming into a clear plan. This process not only aids in prioritization but also in setting realistic goals, helping you focus on what's achievable. The clarity gained from a brain dump can be empowering, providing direction and purpose to your daily activities.

The key to ongoing clarity and organization is maintaining regular brain dump sessions. Consider incorporating this technique into your weekly planning routine as a tool to reset your mind and prepare for the days ahead. Set a regular time each week to perform a brain dump, ensuring it becomes a consistent habit. As you review your lists, update and refine them, allowing room for change and adaptation. This practice keeps your thoughts organized and priorities clear, reducing the mental clutter that can lead to procrastination. Over time, regular brain dumps enhance your productivity, making it easier to tackle tasks confidently.

Remember, the goal isn't to eliminate every thought but to create a system that manages them effectively. With this approach, you transform mental chaos into clarity, paving the way for more focused and intentional actions. As you explore these strategies, you'll discover that breaking down tasks and organizing your thoughts can lead to a more balanced and productive life.

Make a Difference with Your Review

Help Others Take the First Step

"Alone we can do so little; together we can do so much." – Helen Keller

Think about the times you've felt stuck and how much it meant when someone offered a little guidance or inspiration. Now, you have the chance to do that for someone else.

Would you take a moment to help someone like you—someone ready to embrace change but unsure where to begin?

With *Organizing and Cleaning with ADHD*, my goal is to show that creating a calm, functional home is possible, even when life feels overwhelming. But for this message to reach more people who need it, I need your help.

How your review makes an impact: Most people decide which book to buy based on reviews. A quick note from you could be the encouragement they need to take that first step. Your review might help:

- One more person break free from the stress of clutter.

- One more family create a home where everyone can thrive.

- One more individual discover strategies that truly work for their ADHD brain.

- One more life change for the better.

Want to help? It's easy:

Simply scan the QR code to share your thoughts.

Your review doesn't need to be elaborate—just sincere and heartfelt. It could inspire someone to take the first step toward creating a more organized and balanced life. If helping others resonates with you, thank you for taking the time to share your thoughts and make a meaningful impact.

With gratitude,

Avery Holland

Chapter 7

Room-by-Room Organization: Creating Calm from Chaos

Our homes reflect our lives—a mix of chaos and calm, busyness and rest. For those with ADHD, the home can often feel overwhelming, with each room presenting its own set of challenges. From the kitchen that doubles as a family hub to the living room that invites relaxation but also collects clutter, every space has the potential to either support or hinder daily life.

Room-by-room organization is about tackling each area with purpose and intention. Instead of trying to organize the whole house at once (a recipe for overwhelm), breaking it down into manageable sections makes the process achievable and even empowering. This chapter will take you on a guided journey through the spaces that make up your home, offering practical strategies tailored to the unique needs of an ADHD mind.

No matter where you start—whether it's a cluttered pantry, an overflowing laundry room, or a chaotic home office—each room is an opportunity to create a space that works for you. Together, we'll transform the chaos into calm, one step at a time.

7.1 The Kitchen and Pantry: Streamlining the Heart of Your Home

Imagine stepping into your kitchen, where everything has its place, and meal prep feels like a breeze. For many with ADHD, the kitchen can be a hub of chaos, a space where intention meets distraction. Let's turn that around. Creating an intuitive kitchen layout allows you to transform this often-overwhelming area into a sanctuary of efficiency and calm. Start by grouping similar items—baking supplies, breakfast essentials, or spices—and organizing them within easy reach. Think of it as creating a logical flow for your kitchen. For instance:

- Keep pots and pans near the stove.
- Store utensils close to the prep area.
- Arrange items to create a seamless path from ingredient to plate.

This setup saves time and minimizes the mental clutter of searching for tools mid-cooking.

Streamline Meal Prep

Meal prep can quickly become daunting, but it doesn't have to be a chore with the right systems in place. In our home, I use a meal planning journal to organize our weekly meals, planning from Monday to Sunday. After deciding on the meals, I create a detailed grocery list based on the ingredients needed. To streamline shopping, I transfer this list to the "Reminders" app on my phone, which makes it easily accessible. I also share the list with my husband through the app so we can both keep track of what's added or removed, ensuring we avoid doubling up on items or forgetting anything essential. This system keeps meal prep organized and stress-free.

Here are some strategies to further reduce decision fatigue and make meal prep even easier:

- **Use Weekly Meal Planning Templates:** These can streamline your grocery list and reduce the need for daily decisions.

- **Pre-Prep Ingredients:** Chop vegetables, marinate proteins, or portion snacks ahead of time.

- **Set a Dedicated Prep Time:** Block out an hour or two each week to prepare meals or components for the week ahead.

By setting aside a dedicated time to prepare meals in advance, you can enjoy the satisfaction of a home-cooked meal without the stress of last-minute planning.

Tackle Lunch Prep as Part of Your Routine

In our house, we've made a habit of packing school lunches while cooking or during the after-dinner cleanup. Since we're already in the kitchen, it feels like a natural extension of the evening routine:

- Pull out lunchboxes during cleanup.

- Prep simple items like sandwiches, fruits, or snacks.

- Store everything in an easy-to-grab spot for the morning.

This small habit has been a game-changer for our mornings. Instead of scrambling to assemble everything while rushing out the door, we start the day with one less task. The same approach works for packing work lunches or prepping lunch for home—saving time during a busy day so you can focus on work or chores without interruptions.

Declutter and Organize Your Fridge

A cluttered fridge can lead to unnecessary stress, so it's vital to keep it organized. Here's how:

- **Empty and Sort:**
    - Remove everything and group similar items (dairy, condiments, leftovers, etc.).

- Discard expired or spoiled items.

- **Clean and Zone:**

  - Wipe down all shelves and drawers.

  - Designate areas for specific categories:

    - Drinks on the top shelf.

    - Dairy and leftovers in the middle.

    - Raw meats on a tray on the bottom shelf.

    - Fruits and vegetables in their designated drawers.

- **Use Storage Solutions:**

  - Clear bins for smaller items like snacks or condiments.

  - Label items to ensure they are in their proper place when put away.

- **Adopt a Maintenance Habit:**

  - Do a quick check before grocery shopping to discard old items and reorganize.

Organize Your Pantry

A well-organized pantry can make meal prep and cooking significantly easier. Use these steps to create a functional pantry:

- **Declutter:**

  - Empty the shelves and group similar items (snacks, canned goods, baking supplies, etc.).

  - Discard expired food or donate items you won't use.

- **Set Up Zones:**

- Staples like rice and pasta.
- Snacks and quick grabs.
- Canned goods and jars.
- Baking supplies like flour and sugar.

- **Invest in Storage Solutions:**
  - Clear containers for dry goods like flour and cereal.
  - Tiered shelves for canned goods to maximize visibility.
  - Baskets for loose snacks or packets.
  - Door-mounted racks for spices or small items.

- **Label Everything:**
  - Label bins, containers, and shelves to create a system that everyone in the household can follow.

- **Implement FIFO (First-In, First-Out):**
  - Place newer groceries behind older ones to avoid waste.

- **Maintain Monthly:**
  - Dedicate a few minutes monthly to check for expired items and reorganize as needed.

Daily Habits for a Tidy Kitchen

Maintaining a tidy kitchen doesn't have to be overwhelming. Incorporate these quick daily habits:

- Spend five minutes decluttering countertops to keep surfaces clear and ready for action.
- Return items to their designated spots after each use.

- Encourage household members to follow the system using clear labels as visual cues.

By addressing the fridge and pantry with intentional systems and making small, consistent habits part of your routine, you can transform your kitchen into a space that supports—not hinders—your daily life. These changes might take some upfront effort but will pay off in a functional, calm, and welcoming kitchen.

Interactive Element: Create Your Kitchen Command Center

Set up a "Kitchen Command Center" with a weekly meal planner, shopping list, and calendar. To help you get started, scan the QR code at the beginning of this book for free printable tools, including a customizable meal planner and cleaning checklist. Use a magnetic board or wall space to keep these tools visible and accessible, or utilize apps for easy-to-access lists.

This central hub can streamline your kitchen activities, ensuring you are always prepared and organized. Focusing on these strategies can help you create a kitchen that supports your lifestyle, turning meal prep from a source of stress into an opportunity for creativity and nourishment.

7.2 A Clutter-Free Living Room: Relaxation Meets Order

Picture this: a living room that warmly welcomes you, where relaxation isn't just a fleeting idea but an everyday reality. For many, the living room often becomes a catch-all for the clutter of daily life—mail on the coffee table, toys strewn across the floor, or random electronics occupying every surface. Yet, this space holds immense potential to be your sanctuary. Start by embracing the room's role as a hub of comfort and connection.

Transform your living room into a haven of coziness by layering it with soft, inviting touches. Throw pillows and blankets not only add aesthetic appeal but also infuse warmth and texture, turning an ordinary couch into a cozy retreat. Choose colors and patterns that complement your room's palette to create a cohesive look. Incorporating plants or natural elements brings a calming energy indoors. The soothing green hues, the gentle sway of leaves, or even the earthy aroma of fresh flowers can help ground your space and offer a sense of tranquility that counteracts the chaos of daily life.

Managing the inevitable accumulation of items in the living room requires thoughtful organization. Designate specific spots for everyday essentials like remote controls, electronic devices, or even keys. A small tray, decorative bowl, or stylish box can help corral these items, keeping them accessible while avoiding clutter. Decorative baskets work wonders for stowing magazines, blankets, or children's toys. These multi-functional pieces keep things neat and serve as stylish accents that enhance your decor.

Strategic storage solutions can elevate your living room's functionality and aesthetics. Consider furniture with hidden compartments, such as ottomans or coffee tables with drawers, which offer discreet spaces to tuck away board games or other items when not in use. Blanket ladders are a stylish way to display your blankets, transforming them into decorative pieces while keeping your floor space free. Wall-mounted shelves can showcase books or decor while maximizing room in smaller spaces. Select storage options that blend seamlessly with your room's design, ensuring that organization feels like an intentional part of the decor rather than an afterthought.

To maintain this sense of order, build habits that support a clutter-free environment. Schedule regular decluttering sessions, such as a quick weekly sweep, to remove items that don't belong or are no longer needed. This habit keeps clutter from building up and helps the space remain peaceful and functional. Rotating seasonal decor is another effective way to refresh your living room without overcrowding it. Swapping out pillows, throws, or accent pieces with each season keeps the space dynamic while preventing it from feeling stagnant or overly busy.

Enhance your organization efforts with visual systems that simplify cleanup and make staying organized intuitive for everyone in the household. For example, use color-coded bins to separate toys, books, or magazines, making it easier for family members—especially children—to know where things go. Label storage boxes clearly to ensure that even hidden items are easy to locate. These small steps create an environment where tidying up becomes effortless, reinforcing the sense of order and relaxation you've cultivated.

Ultimately, your living room should reflect both style and functionality, serving as a space that invites you to unwind while accommodating the realities of daily life. By combining thoughtful organization, cozy decor, and regular maintenance, you can transform this common area into a retreat that brings comfort and calm to your home.

7.3 Bedroom Bliss: Creating a Restful Retreat

Think about stepping into your bedroom at the end of a long, hectic day. Ideally, it should feel like a warm embrace—a place where the weight of the world falls away, stress melts, and tranquility takes over. To create this kind of restful retreat, start with a calming and minimalist design that sets the tone for relaxation. Neutral color palettes, such as soft grays, calming blues, or gentle creams, provide a serene backdrop that soothes the mind. These colors not only make the space visually cohesive but also foster a sense of calm and balance. Minimalist decor doesn't mean stripping the room of personality; instead, it's about paring down to the essentials that bring joy and peace. A favorite piece of art, a cozy throw blanket, or a softly glowing bedside lamp can add warmth and character without overwhelming the space, ensuring every detail contributes to the room's inviting atmosphere.

Organizing your clothing is crucial to maintaining a tidy and serene bedroom. A cluttered wardrobe can easily spill over into the room, disrupting the visual serenity and creating unnecessary stress. Consider adopting a seasonal wardrobe rotation to keep things manageable and organized. Store off-season clothes in bins under the bed, in vacuum-sealed bags, or on high shelves, freeing up prime closet space for your current wardrobe. Drawer organizers can turn chaotic drawers into neatly segmented areas where everything has its place, making it easier to find socks, underwear, or accessories without rummaging. These simple solutions create a sense of order that extends beyond the closet, preserving the peaceful energy of the entire room while saving time and reducing frustration during busy mornings.

Maintaining the inviting nature of your bedroom requires consistent care, but it doesn't have to be overwhelming. Start with a small daily habit like making your bed. This seemingly minor task takes just a few minutes yet establishes a tone of order and accomplishment for the day ahead. Pair this with a weekly routine of dusting surfaces, wiping down furniture, and vacuuming to prevent allergens and dust from accumulating. These regular cleaning rituals ensure your bedroom feels fresh and welcoming at all times. Walking into a clean, tidy space at the end of the day creates an immediate sense of relief and relaxation, reinforcing the room's role as a personal retreat.

Improving your sleep quality is another essential aspect of a restful bedroom. Small, thoughtful changes can make a big difference. For example, introduce blackout curtains or a sleep mask to create total darkness, promoting deeper, uninterrupted sleep. Aromatherapy can also be incredibly effective in fostering relaxation; diffuse calming scents like lavender, chamomile, or sandalwood to soothe the senses and prepare your body for rest. If noise tends to disrupt your sleep, a white noise machine or a soothing soundscape can mask unwanted sounds, enveloping you in a peaceful auditory environment. Even adjusting the temperature slightly cooler can improve your sleep, as cooler conditions encourage the body to relax more naturally. Together, these strategies can turn your bedroom into a haven where rest and rejuvenation come effortlessly.

Ultimately, designing a bedroom that fosters relaxation is about creating a balance between comfort, functionality, and personal style. It's a space that reflects calmness and simplicity, prioritizing only what adds value to your peace of mind. By incorporating thoughtful design, smart organization, and habits that maintain cleanliness, you can transform your bedroom into a true sanctuary—a personal retreat where you can escape the chaos of the day and recharge for the challenges ahead.

7.4 Streamlining Bathrooms: Easy Cleanup Routines

Stepping into a well-organized bathroom can feel like a small but meaningful act of self-care, offering a moment of peace amid the chaos of daily life. However, bathrooms are often prone to clutter, especially when space is limited. Maximizing storage in a small bathroom requires thoughtful solutions that make the most of every inch. Over-the-door organizers are an excellent way to store toiletries like hairbrushes, styling tools, or extra soaps, keeping them accessible without crowding countertops. Stackable bins or tiered organizers can transform the under-sink area into a functional space, allowing you to separate cleaning supplies, spare toiletries, and extra towels. Floating shelves or corner racks can also help utilize vertical space, offering additional storage for everyday essentials like hand towels or decorative items. These solutions ensure every item has its place, reducing visual clutter and streamlining your morning routine.

Maintaining a clean and tidy bathroom isn't just about aesthetics—it sets the tone for your day. A fresh, organized bathroom can have a calming effect, while a messy or grimy one may add unnecessary stress. Adopting a consistent cleaning routine makes upkeep manageable. Start with a bi-weekly deep clean, focusing on high-impact tasks such as scrubbing tiles, disinfecting countertops, wiping down faucets, and washing bath mats. This prevents dirt and grime from building up, keeping your bathroom hygienic and pleasant. Incorporate quick daily habits as well: wipe down mirrors and sinks after use, shake out bathmats to remove debris, and empty the trash regularly. These small actions, done consistently, create a cumulative effect that ensures your bathroom always feels fresh and inviting without requiring hours of effort.

Bathrooms can also become the final resting place for forgotten products, from half-used bottles of shampoo to expired skincare items. Regularly decluttering personal care items is essential to maintaining a functional and streamlined bathroom. Commit to a monthly check of expiration dates on skincare, cosmetics, and medicines, discarding anything past its prime. Use this opportunity to evaluate your products: ask yourself if each item genuinely enhances your daily routine or simply takes up space. Group similar items together as you organize, creating zones for haircare, skincare, and everyday essentials. This practice ensures you keep only what you use, freeing up space and making your bathroom more enjoyable to use.

Organization is the backbone of an efficient bathroom. Small tools like drawer dividers can work wonders for creating order within drawers and categorizing items like makeup, grooming tools, or first-aid supplies. Shower caddies with built-in compartments keep shampoos, conditioners, and body wash neatly arranged and within reach, preventing a jumble of bottles from dominating the shower area. Consider using clear bins or labeled containers for under-sink storage, which not only make it easy to locate what you need but also help family members return items to their proper place. Lazy Susans or turntables are another clever solution for storing smaller items like skincare or medicines, providing quick access without rummaging. By investing in organization systems tailored to your needs, you simplify your daily routine and create a bathroom environment that fosters calm and efficiency.

Don't forget to add a touch of personality to your bathroom while keeping it functional. Small details like a matching set of hand towels, a stylish soap dispenser, or a plant that thrives in humidity can elevate the space and make it feel more intentional. If you're anything like me, keeping plants alive might feel like one more thing to worry about. Thankfully, artificial plants have come a long way—they look incredibly realistic and only need a quick wipe-down now and then. With thoughtful design, consistent maintenance, and smart storage solutions, your bathroom can transform from a cluttered utility space into a sanctuary of cleanliness and order—a place where you can begin and end your day with ease and tranquility.

7.5 Tackling the Home Office: Enhancing Productivity

Picture your home office, which should be a productivity hub yet often becomes a battlefield of distractions. Creating a workspace that minimizes interruptions is crucial for maintaining focus, especially when dealing with ADHD. Start by positioning your desk away from windows or high-traffic areas, reducing the temptation to glance outside or engage in unrelated activities. Integrating noise-canceling headphones into your workspace can dramatically enhance your ability to concentrate by isolating you from distracting sounds. This strategic move crafts a sanctuary of focus, empowering you to immerse fully in your tasks, undisturbed by the chaos of the outside world.

Your office layout plays a significant role in how productive you feel. Ergonomic furniture isn't just about comfort; it's about ensuring your body supports your mind's efforts. A chair that encourages good posture and a desk at the right height can prevent strain and keep you comfortable during long work sessions. Keep frequently used supplies within arm's reach to reduce time spent searching for that elusive pen or sticky note. This accessibility streamlines your workflow, allowing you to maintain momentum and focus on the task at hand. Consider using desk organizers or drawer dividers to keep these items neatly arranged, preventing clutter from creeping in.

Digital clutter can be as distracting as physical mess, so it's essential to manage it effectively. Setting up a digital filing system can transform how you interact with your computer. Create folders for different projects and ensure your desktop remains free of unnecessary icons. Regularly clearing your desktop enhances visual appeal and reduces mental clutter, helping you start each day with a fresh slate. Bookmark frequently visited sites for easy access, reducing the time spent typing in addresses and minimizing the risk of falling down internet rabbit holes.

Maintaining a tidy workspace requires habits that support organization. Begin each day by tidying your desk and putting away any accumulated stray papers or items. This simple action sets a tone of order and readiness. Consider implementing a "clean desk" policy at the end of each day, ensuring everything is in place before you leave. This routine creates a welcoming environment for the next day, reducing the morning scramble and allowing you to dive straight into work.

Interactive Element: Personalized Workspace Layout Plan

Take a moment to sketch your current office layout. Identify areas where clutter accumulates or distractions occur. Strategize how you can rearrange furniture or supplies to minimize these issues. Create a plan that reflects your needs and enhances your productivity, considering both physical setup and digital organization.

These strategies help create a home office that genuinely supports your productivity, offering a space where focus and efficiency thrive.

7.6 Laundry Room Logic: Tackling the Tumbles

Transforming the often-overlooked laundry room into a pivotal area for household efficiency begins with establishing sorting stations for various types of laundry. Allocating distinct bins for whites, colors, and delicates simplifies load management and promotes household participation, making laundry a collective endeavor rather than an individual task. Installing wall hooks and shelves enhances organization and accessibility, with shelves storing detergents and cleaning products and hooks offering spots for hanging items such as cleaning brushes or drying racks. These measures utilize space effectively and instill a sense of order, easing the laundry routine.

Practical storage solutions can transform the laundry room from a cluttered space into an organized haven. Use labeled jars or containers to store detergents, softeners, and other laundry essentials. Labels provide clarity, ensuring you grab the right product every time, even during a hectic morning rush. Vertical storage solutions are beneficial for tight spaces. Consider installing a wall-mounted rack for brooms and mops, freeing up floor space and keeping the area tidy. These little adjustments enhance functionality and contribute to a visually pleasing environment, making laundry day feel less daunting.

Streamlining your laundry routine can save you time and stress. Scheduling specific laundry days helps manage loads without letting them pile up. Choose two or three days a week when you'll focus on laundry, allowing you to stay on top of things without feeling overwhelmed. Pairing laundry with other household tasks can boost efficiency—perhaps folding clothes while watching a favorite show or listening to a podcast. This multitasking approach turns laundry from a mundane duty into a more enjoyable experience, integrating it seamlessly into your weekly rhythm.

A clutter-free laundry area is crucial for maintaining efficiency. Start by removing unnecessary items to maximize the workspace. If your laundry room doubles as a storage area, consider what truly needs to be there.

Consider donating or relocating items that serve no immediate purpose in the laundry process. A small basket for stray socks or single items can keep your space tidy, preventing clutter from accumulating in corners. This attention to detail enhances the room's functionality and creates a more inviting atmosphere, making laundry less of a chore and more manageable.

Organizing your laundry room with these strategies ensures it serves its purpose effectively, supporting your household's needs without adding to the chaos. With these systems in place, you spend less time searching for supplies and more time enjoying the results—a clean, refreshed wardrobe ready for whatever life throws your way. As you wrap up your efforts in this often-overlooked space, you can turn your attention to the next chapter, where we'll explore digital decluttering and management, helping you apply similar principles to your virtual spaces.

Transform Your Home, One Room at a Time

Discover easy-to-follow strategies tailored to ADHD minds to create functional, calm, and welcoming spaces.

KITCHEN & PANTRY
STREAMLINE MEAL PREP & CREATE ORDER

- **Group items by category:** Keep baking supplies, snacks, or breakfast essentials together.
- **Designate zones:** Pots and pans near the stove, utensils by the prep area.
- Use clear containers for pantry items with labels for easy identification.
- Introduce FIFO (First-In, First-Out) to reduce waste and ensure older items are used first.

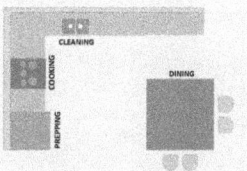

LIVING ROOM
RELAXATION MEETS FUNCTIONALITY

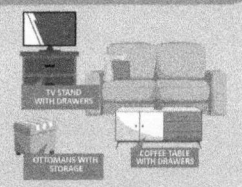

- **Choose multi-functional furniture:** Ottomans with storage, coffee tables with drawers.
- Use decorative baskets for toys, magazines, or blankets.
- Create a designated spot for remote controls and electronic devices.
- Rotate seasonal decor to keep the space fresh and uncluttered.

BEDROOM
RESTFUL RETREATS BEGIN WITH ORGANIZATION

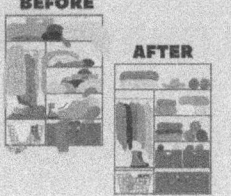

- Adopt a seasonal wardrobe rotation to keep closets manageable.
- Use drawer organizers for socks, underwear, and accessories.
- Incorporate calming elements like neutral colors, blackout curtains, and aromatherapy diffusers.
- Maintain a daily habit of making the bed to set a tone of order.

HOME OFFICE
PRODUCTIVITY STARTS WITH A TIDY WORKSPACE

- Position your desk away from distractions like windows or high-traffic areas.
- Use drawer dividers or desktop organizers for pens, sticky notes, and chargers.
- Create a digital filing system to reduce desktop clutter.
- Establish a "clean desk" policy at the end of each day to reset for the next.

BATHROOM
STREAMLINE AND SIMPLIFY

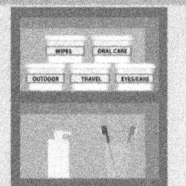

- Maximize vertical space with floating shelves or over-the-door organizers.
- Use clear/stackable bins or tiered organizers under the sink for toiletries.
- Regularly declutter expired products (e.g., skincare, medicines).
- Incorporate calming elements like matching towels or decorative soap dispensers.

LAUNDRY ROOM
EFFICIENCY IN EVERY LOAD

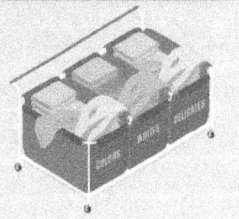

- Use labeled bins for whites, colors, and delicates to simplify sorting.
- Mount shelves or racks for detergents and cleaning supplies to save space.
- Keep a basket for stray socks or single items.
- Schedule regular laundry days to prevent piles from becoming overwhelming.

SMALL STEPS, BIG CHANGES

You don't need to organize everything at once. Start with one room, one tip, one change. These small efforts add up to a home that supports your lifestyle and brings you peace.

Chapter 8

Digital Declutter and Management

Picture this: your digital life feels like a messy desk piled high with papers, making it difficult to find anything when needed. For many of us, our digital spaces mirror the physical clutter we strive to control—emails overflow, files scattered across desktops, and important documents seem to vanish just when we need them most. This digital chaos isn't just frustrating; it can weigh heavily on our minds, adding unnecessary stress and making it difficult to focus. The good news is that organizing your digital environment can bring clarity and calm, transforming it into a space that supports rather than hinders your daily life.

Digital organization is more than just cleaning up your desktop—it's about creating a system that reduces mental clutter and streamlines access to the information you need. A clutter-free digital environment can significantly enhance productivity, allowing you to work more efficiently without the distraction of a messy workspace. Organizing your digital files lets you quickly find what you're looking for, saving time and reducing stress. This makes your work more productive and gives you more time for the things you love.

Organize Your Files

To start decluttering your digital life, consider adopting a systematic approach to file organization. Begin by creating a structured folder hierarchy that makes sense for your needs. Think of it like organizing a library, where each book has its place on the shelf. Start with broad categories and break them down into more specific subfolders. For instance, you might have a main folder for "Work" divided into projects or clients, each with its own subfolder. Regularly purging unnecessary files is also crucial. Set aside time, perhaps once a month, to review and delete no longer relevant files, helping to maintain a tidy digital space and prevent it from becoming overwhelming.

Tame Your Inbox

Emails are another area where clutter can quickly accumulate, and I know firsthand how easy it is to let this get out of control. I'll admit, I'm guilty of signing up for promotions to snag a discount, only to ignore the endless follow-up emails. Instead of unsubscribing, I'd spend time every day deleting them—a temporary fix that didn't solve the problem. Sound familiar? If so, it's time to break the cycle.

Start by unsubscribing from promotional emails you no longer want. Most emails include an "unsubscribe" link at the bottom—click it! Tools like Unroll.me can help you identify and unsubscribe from multiple mailing lists in one go for quicker results. By clearing out unnecessary emails, you'll reduce the volume of incoming clutter and make your inbox more straightforward to manage.

Once you've trimmed the excess, set up filters and labels to organize important emails automatically; for example, you can create folders for bills, work correspondence, or personal messages and use filters to send emails directly to the appropriate folder. This way, you can focus on what matters without sifting through irrelevant messages.

Adopt a Daily Email Routine

To maintain a clean inbox, consider implementing a daily email routine. Dedicate just five minutes each day to reviewing, responding to, or sorting new messages. Archive or delete anything no longer needed, and use labels to keep the rest organized. This small habit prevents your inbox from becoming overwhelming and ensures you stay on top of important correspondence.

Use the Right Tools

Numerous tools are available to assist in digital decluttering. File management apps, like Google Drive or Dropbox, can help you organize and access your files seamlessly. Email clients like Outlook or Gmail offer advanced sorting features, enabling you to organize and manage emails more efficiently, which can save time and reduce stress. Explore these options to find the ones that work best for your needs and make managing your digital life easier.

Declutter Your Digital Life Beyond Files and Emails

Digital decluttering isn't just about inboxes and files. Consider taking stock of your social media accounts, apps, and subscriptions. Unfollow accounts that no longer add value to your life, delete apps you rarely use, and cancel subscriptions you don't need. Simplifying these aspects of your digital life can free up mental bandwidth and create a sense of control.

These tools can streamline your digital life, reducing clutter and making it easier to focus on what matters.

With a clean inbox, organized files, and a streamlined digital environment, you'll feel more focused and in control of your digital spaces. Small steps like unsubscribing from unnecessary emails or creating structured folders may seem minor, but they significantly reduce stress and improve efficiency. By taking the time to declutter digitally, you're making a space that supports your productivity and brings peace of mind—no matter how hectic life gets.

Interactive Element: Digital Declutter Checklist

Create a Digital Declutter Checklist to guide your organizational efforts. Start with a list of tasks such as setting up folder hierarchies, implementing email filters, and scheduling regular file purges. Use this checklist to track your progress and maintain a clutter-free digital environment. This visual tool helps keep you organized and provides a tangible reminder of your accomplishments in maintaining digital order.

By approaching digital decluttering with intention and consistency, you can transform your online space into one that supports your goals and reduces stress. A clear digital landscape can enhance focus, boost productivity, and provide a sense of calm, much like an organized physical space.

8.1 Managing Digital Distractions: Focus in a Digital World

In today's fast-paced digital world, distractions are as omnipresent as the devices in our hands. Have you ever sat down to work only to be pulled away by the ding of a social media notification or the relentless ping of email alerts? These interruptions fragment your attention and drain your energy, leaving you feeling frazzled rather than focused. Social media is a major player in this distraction game, with platforms designed to capture your attention and keep you scrolling. The constant flow of information can be overwhelming, making it difficult to concentrate on tasks.

Similarly, frequent email alerts can create a sense of urgency, pulling you away from important work to manage an ever-expanding inbox. It's like trying to read a book with someone tapping you on the shoulder every few minutes. These digital distractions can impede productivity and make it challenging to maintain focus, especially for those with ADHD, where attention is already a precious commodity.

So, how can you reclaim your focus and minimize these interruptions? One effective strategy is to use apps that block distracting websites. Tools like Freedom or Cold Turkey can prevent you from accessing sites that sap your time and attention. Setting up these digital barriers creates a focused environment that allows you to concentrate on your priorities. Think of it as putting up a "do not disturb" sign in your digital world, giving you the space to work without unnecessary distractions. Another approach is to use the "Do Not Disturb" mode on your devices during work sessions. This setting silences notifications, letting you dive deep into your tasks without being pulled away by the latest post or update. It's a simple yet powerful way to focus on what matters most.

Scheduling specific times to check emails and messages can also help manage digital distractions. Instead of reacting to each alert as it comes in, set designated periods throughout the day to review and respond to communications. This practice reduces interruptions and allows you to engage with your emails and messages more mindfully, ensuring you address each one with the attention it deserves. Think of it as creating a daily appointment with your inbox, giving you control over when and how you interact with it. By establishing these boundaries, you prevent your devices from dictating your schedule and regain control over your time.

Integrating these strategies into your routine can significantly enhance your ability to focus in a digital world. However, remember, it's about finding the right balance. Not every strategy will work for everyone, so it's important to experiment and discover what suits your lifestyle and needs. Personalization is at the heart of effective digital distraction management. Whether it's blocking social media during work hours or setting a specific time for emails, tailor these approaches to fit your unique situation. As you explore these methods, you'll find that reducing digital distractions boosts productivity and enhances overall well-being, creating a calmer, more intentional digital experience.

8.2 Using Apps and Tools for ADHD-Friendly Organization

In today's tech-driven world, apps and digital tools have become indispensable allies for managing life's chaos, especially when ADHD is part of the equation. The design of these digital companions is to address specific organizational needs, making them perfect for those seeking structure amid the whirlwind of distractions. Here's how you can incorporate some of these tools into your life:

- **Task Management Apps**: Task management apps, such as **Todoist**, **Asana**, or **Trello**, are handy for managing daily responsibilities.

- Many of these apps feature visual reminders that help you keep track of tasks without feeling overwhelmed.

- Imagine having a virtual assistant like Todoist gently nudging you when it's time to switch gears or finish a task. This can revolutionize how individuals grappling with forgetfulness or procrastination manage their daily tasks.

- **Digital Note-Taking Tools**: Digital note-taking tools with audio integration, such as **Evernote** or **Microsoft OneNote**, offer a unique advantage.

  - They allow you to capture fleeting thoughts or ideas on the go, ensuring that nothing gets lost in the shuffle.

  - Features like voice memos make it easy to record your thoughts when typing feels cumbersome, simplifying the process of organizing ideas later.

- **Digital Planners**: Digital planners, like **Google Calendar**, **Notion**, or **GoodNotes**, are fantastic resources worth exploring.

  - These tools help track tasks and manage time more effectively.

  - With customizable templates for daily planning, you can tailor your schedule to fit your unique needs, whether you prefer minimalist layouts or detailed systems.

  - Syncing capabilities allow you to access your schedule across multiple devices, ensuring your plans are always within reach—whether at home, work, or on the go.

- **Habit-Tracking Features**: Apps like **Habitica**, **Streaks**, or **Momentum** include features that support habit tracking.

  - These tools provide visual cues, such as charts or progress bars, giving you a clear picture of your progress.

  - This transforms the abstract concept of habit-building into something concrete and measurable, boosting motivation.

When choosing the right tools, it's crucial to consider your individual needs and preferences:

- A user-friendly interface can make all the difference in how often you use an app. If navigating the tool feels intuitive, you're more likely to incorporate it into your routine regularly.

- Take advantage of free trials offered by many productivity apps to explore different functionalities and determine which ones enhance your workflow. Apps like **ClickUp** or **Monday.com** often provide trial periods.

Community recommendations and reviews also offer valuable insights into the effectiveness of certain apps. Hearing about others' experiences can guide you in making informed decisions and help you avoid tools that might not be a good fit. Remember, there's no one-size-fits-all solution—experimenting is essential to finding what works best for you.

Ultimately, the key to successful organization lies in personalizing your approach. Integrating these digital tools into your daily life allows you to create a system that complements your lifestyle and supports your goals. These apps are not just about managing tasks—they're about empowering you to take control of your time and focus, ensuring you have the resources to thrive in a world full of distractions. So, explore the possibilities, embrace the technology that works for you, and watch your days become more organized and less stressful.

8.3 Creating a Minimalist Digital Life

Envision opening your device to find a clean, uncluttered screen where only the essentials reside. This simplicity creates an inviting atmosphere, offering a sense of liberation and openness. Adopting a minimalist digital lifestyle can bring about this sense of clarity and efficiency. When you strip away digital clutter, mental clarity emerges, reducing the decision fatigue that often comes with too many choices. It becomes easier to use technology when interactions are simplified, allowing you to focus on what truly matters.

To embrace digital minimalism, start by minimizing the number of apps and programs you use. Each app you download is like a new resident in your digital home, demanding attention and space. Decide which ones add value to your life and let go of the rest. Regularly declutter subscriptions and feeds, too. Unsubscribe from newsletters you never read, and unfollow accounts that no longer align with your interests. This ongoing practice keeps your digital space clean and ensures that what's left is meaningful and relevant.

Intentional digital usage isn't just about cutting back; it's about engaging mindfully with your devices. Set limits on screen time and app usage to prevent digital overwhelm. Instead of mindlessly scrolling through social media or binge-watching videos, choose quality content that enriches your life. Opt for articles that inspire, documentaries that teach, or apps that aid productivity. By being selective, you create a digital environment that supports growth and well-being.

Incorporating digital minimalism into daily routines can create lasting change. Schedule regular digital detox periods to reset your focus and energy. For instance, you could set aside a weekend for a complete break from screens, allowing your mind to recharge. Establish digital curfews and give yourself permission to unplug in the evening hours. These breaks can foster deeper connections with those around you and provide the mental space needed for creativity and thought. Creating a digital diet plan can also help you consume technology more consciously. Decide when and how you'll engage with devices, ensuring they serve your needs without taking over your life.

Digital detoxes are more than just trendy buzzwords; they are vital for maintaining balance in a tech-saturated world. Engaging in weekend digital detox challenges can be a fun and refreshing way to disconnect. These challenges encourage you to spend time with the people you love, get outdoors, read a book, or enjoy a hobby without the constant interruption of screens. Scheduling screen-free hours each day can also be beneficial. These windows of tech-free time allow you to engage more fully with the world around you, boosting your mood and improving your overall well-being.

As we navigate this digital age, remember that technology is a tool meant to enhance our lives—not dominate them. By adopting a minimalist approach, you reclaim your digital space and craft an environment that aligns with your values and goals. This chapter's exploration of digital minimalism highlights how small changes can significantly improve clarity and focus. It's about finding a balance that works for you and creating a digital life that supports your journey toward a more organized and fulfilling existence. As we move forward, let's consider how these principles can be applied beyond the digital realm, shaping our physical spaces and habits as we seek order and peace.

Chapter 9

Gamification and Creative Approaches

Have you ever been so immersed in a game that you don't even notice how much time has passed? Whether leveling up in a video game or winning a board game with friends, gamification taps into something powerful within us. Now, imagine channeling that same energy into cleaning and organizing your home. It sounds intriguing, doesn't it? Gamification involves applying game-design elements to everyday tasks, making them more engaging and less of a chore. This approach is especially beneficial for individuals with ADHD, whose brains often seek immediate rewards and engagement to stay motivated and focused. By transforming mundane chores into exciting challenges, you can turn cleaning into an experience that feels more like play than work.

Gamification can be as simple as using a point system for completed tasks. Think of each chore as a quest, where every task earns points. You might decide that tidying up the living room is worth ten points and cleaning the bathroom, which is a more intensive task, is worth twenty. These points can accumulate toward a reward of your choice—a treat like a favorite snack, a movie night, or a leisurely afternoon with a book. If you live with family or roommates, consider creating a friendly competition by setting up a leaderboard. Everyone can track their progress and compete for small prizes, adding a social element that makes cleaning more fun and collaborative.

One of the joys of gamification is the ability to incorporate imaginative challenges into your cleaning routine. Consider organizing a timed "tidy-up" race, where you set a timer and see who can clean their designated area the fastest. Adding an element of urgency and excitement makes a routine task into a thrilling game. Another idea is a scavenger hunt, where participants search for and put away misplaced items around the house. This helps with tidying up and engages your problem-solving skills, making the process more stimulating and enjoyable. The key is to find what excites you and makes cleaning feel less like a chore.

The psychological benefits of gamification are significant. Turning tasks into games reduces their perceived difficulty, making them more approachable. Achieving small goals, like earning points or completing challenges, releases dopamine in the brain. As mentioned earlier, this neurotransmitter is associated with pleasure and reward, which explains why finishing a task can feel so satisfying. Gamification encourages a positive association with cleaning, transforming it from a dreaded obligation into a rewarding activity. It helps shift your perspective, allowing you to view chores as opportunities for achievement rather than burdens.

To set up gamified tasks, start by identifying what motivates you. Apps that track and reward task completion can be a great tool, providing structure and instant feedback. You might also create themed cleaning days with specific challenges, such as "Laundry Olympics" or "Kitchen Konquest." These themes add variety to your routine, keeping it fresh and engaging. Tailoring the gamification process to your interests and preferences is important, ensuring it remains enjoyable and sustainable. By incorporating these elements into your cleaning routine, you can transform how you approach household tasks, making them something to look forward to rather than dread.

9.1 Using Apps to Gamify Your Cleaning Routine

In a world where technology touches nearly every part of our lives, it's no surprise that apps have emerged as powerful tools to transform the way we approach cleaning. Imagine an app that turns your cleaning tasks into engaging adventures, complete with levels to conquer and rewards to earn. This is the essence of gamification in the digital age, where apps track your progress and provide rewards, making organizing less of an obligation and more of an exciting game. Platforms offering structured cleaning challenges can add an element of fun, motivating you to tackle tasks with enthusiasm.

Take Habitica, for example, an app that cleverly turns your daily chores into quests within a role-playing game. As you complete tasks in real life, your in-game character earns gold, experience points, and items. Habitica's design caters to the unique needs of those with ADHD, offering visual progress tracking, automatic task repetition, and customizable avatars, all of which enhance motivation by making chores feel like part of an epic adventure. Another app, Tody, visualizes cleaning tasks as game levels, helping you see your progress and feel a sense of accomplishment as you move through your cleaning goals. Tody's interface is simple and intuitive, providing reminders and prompts to keep you on track, ensuring that cleaning becomes a consistent part of your routine.

Integrating these apps into your cleaning routine can revolutionize the way you approach organization. They offer reminders and prompts that help maintain consistency, a crucial factor for anyone trying to establish new habits. The visual progress tracking and achievement badges provide instant feedback, tapping into the brain's reward system and boosting motivation. These apps turn mundane tasks into rewarding experiences, making sticking with your cleaning schedule easier over the long term.

When selecting an app to gamify your cleaning routine, consider what features best align with your preferences and goals. Try out multiple apps to see which interface resonates with you. Some people prefer a clean, minimalist design, while others enjoy a more colorful, interactive experience. Pay attention to the app's usability: Are the features intuitive? Do the reminders fit into your daily life? The right app will feel like a natural extension of your routine, making it a valuable ally in keeping your home organized.

The benefits of these apps extend beyond mere task completion. They bring a sense of playfulness to cleaning, turning it into an activity to enjoy rather than avoid. By engaging with these tools, you can transform your perspective on chores, turning them into opportunities for achievement and enjoyment. Through the gamification lens, cleaning becomes more than just a necessity; it becomes an enriching part of your day.

9.2 Creative Organizing Techniques for ADHD Minds

Envision stepping into a room where every object narrates its own tale. This transcends mere organization—it's a form of visual storytelling that breathes life into your surroundings. For many with ADHD, traditional organizing methods can feel stifling. But by using creative approaches that cater to your strengths, organizing becomes not only manageable but enjoyable. Visual storytelling through organizing means letting your space speak for you. It's about arranging items to reflect your personality and passions. Consider using color and texture to differentiate storage areas. Bright bins for craft supplies, textured baskets for blankets—each choice adds a layer of personal expression to your home. This method helps with organization and turns your environment into a vibrant reflection of who you are.

Let's explore some creative organizing solutions that transform spaces into personal galleries. Imagine displaying your collection of hats or jewelry as part of the decor, hanging them on hooks, or arranging them on a stylish stand. Not only does this keep them organized, but it also adds a unique flair to your room. Or consider arranging books by color on shelves, as this will create a visually striking effect and make finding what you need easier. The rainbow of spines becomes a focal point, turning your bookshelf into an art piece. These creative solutions offer a way to organize that feels less like a chore and more like an opportunity for artistic expression.

The benefits of these creative techniques are profound. They leverage your natural creativity, turning organizing into a form of self-expression. By personalizing your space, you reduce the boredom often associated with traditional methods. Organizing becomes a dynamic process that evolves with your tastes and interests. This approach encourages you to see your environment through a creative lens, making the process more engaging and less of a dreaded task. It's about finding joy in the act of organizing, allowing your space to tell your story.

To integrate creativity into your organizing, start by experimenting with different layouts and arrangements. Move things around, try new configurations, and see what feels right. Maybe that chair belongs in a different corner, or your desk would work better facing the window. The key is to keep experimenting until your space feels just right. Incorporate art projects into your organizing tasks. Paint a mural on a wall or create a collage of photos and mementos. These projects add a personal touch, making your space uniquely yours. By embracing creativity, you open the door to endless possibilities, transforming your home into a place of inspiration and comfort.

9.3 Reward Systems: Motivating Through Incentives

Imagine the feeling of crossing a task off your list, knowing a reward awaits at the finish line. This is the power of incentives. They act as motivators, making the journey through chores and organizing efforts more enjoyable and purposeful. Rewards tap into our natural desire for pleasure, driving us to complete tasks with enthusiasm. The concept of immediate versus delayed gratification comes into play here. Immediate rewards provide instant satisfaction and feedback, like taking a quick coffee break after tidying up the kitchen. They cater to the brain's craving for instant results, especially for those with ADHD, who might find it challenging to wait for long-term rewards. On the other hand, delayed gratification involves working toward a larger reward, such as collecting points toward a desired purchase, like a new book or gadget. This approach can teach patience and build self-discipline, offering a sense of achievement that grows over time.

When setting up a reward system, you must choose incentives that genuinely excite and motivate you. After completing a task list, consider earning a leisure activity, such as watching an episode of your favorite show. Now, productivity has turned into a gateway to relaxation and enjoyment. Alternatively, create a points system where each completed task earns points toward a larger goal. Perhaps a weekend getaway or a coveted tech gadget. This system not only motivates you to tackle your to-do list but also adds a layer of excitement and anticipation to routine tasks. The key is to tailor these rewards to your interests and goals, ensuring they align with what truly brings you joy.

The psychology behind rewards is fascinating and deeply rooted in how our brains function. Completing a task and receiving a reward triggers the release of dopamine. This chemical reaction creates a sense of achievement and progress, reinforcing positive behavior and motivating you to continue. It's like a feedback loop where each completed task leads to a reward, which in turn fuels your desire to accomplish more. Over time, this cycle can transform your approach to organizing, making it not only a necessity but an activity to look forward to.

Implementing an effective reward system involves some thoughtful planning. Start by identifying tasks that you find challenging or tedious, then pair them with rewards that feel proportionate to the effort required. The reward must match the difficulty of the task to maintain a sense of fairness and satisfaction. For example, a small task like organizing a drawer might earn a quick break, while a more extensive project like decluttering a room gains a more substantial reward. Keep the system flexible and adaptable, adjusting the rewards as your interests and goals evolve. This ensures the system remains engaging and effective in the long run, continuously motivating you to tackle tasks and maintain an organized space.

9.4 Incorporating Music and Movement in Cleaning Routines

Have you ever experienced the transformative power of music, how a single track can uplift your spirits or breathe life into a mundane task? Music has an uncanny ability to energize and elevate our spirits, turning the same old tasks into enjoyable experiences. When it comes to cleaning, music can be your secret weapon. Imagine curating playlists with upbeat or motivational tracks that turn your cleaning routine into a mini dance party. The rhythm of the music acts as a motivator, helping you stay on track and making the process feel less like a chore. By setting the tempo of your cleaning to the beat of your favorite songs, you can transform the vibe of your entire environment.

Consider how dancing while vacuuming or mopping can turn a straightforward chore into a workout session. Not only does this make cleaning more enjoyable, but it also provides a way to incorporate physical activity into your daily routine. You can get your heart rate up, burn some calories, and have fun simultaneously. Singing along during repetitive tasks, like folding laundry or scrubbing counters, adds an element of joy and creativity. These musical moments help you maintain focus, making it easier to complete tasks without feeling overwhelmed. Music has the power to make time fly, and before you know it, you've accomplished more than you anticipated.

Movement-based cleaning strategies can enhance this experience by making cleaning a dynamic activity. Consider cleaning a form of exercise that keeps your home in order and keeps you moving. Incorporating stretching or yoga breaks throughout your cleaning session can keep your body limber and your mind relaxed. These breaks offer a chance to pause and recharge, preventing fatigue and promoting overall well-being. By viewing cleaning as a holistic activity that benefits both your space and your body, you can find more satisfaction in the process.

To create a dynamic cleaning environment:

1. Take a moment to set up your space in a way that encourages music and movement.

2. Ensure your cleaning supplies are easily accessible and can be moved freely without interruption.

3. Consider investing in a portable speaker or using headphones to immerse yourself in your chosen playlist without distractions.

4. Arrange your cleaning route strategically to flow seamlessly from one task to the next, maintaining your momentum.

Creating an environment that supports music and movement can elevate your cleaning routine into a sensory experience that engages both body and mind.

As we explore these creative approaches to cleaning and organizing, remember that the goal is to create an enjoyable and sustainable routine. Whether through music, movement, or innovative strategies, the key is to find what resonates with you. Embrace these techniques to transform your space and approach to cleaning into something that enhances your life rather than detracts from it. Keep these ideas in mind as we move forward, ready to discover even more ways to make your home a place of joy and comfort.

Chapter 10

Engaging with Family and Support Networks

Sometimes, it can feel like you're speaking a different language from your family when it comes to your ADHD. You try to explain why the clutter seems to multiply or why focusing feels like trying to see through fog, but it sometimes feels like they don't get it. Communication is the bridge to understanding, yet it can be one of the trickiest hurdles to overcome. ADHD doesn't just affect those with it; it weaves into the fabric of family dynamics, influencing how we interact with loved ones. Opening up about these challenges can feel daunting, but it is a pivotal step in fostering a home environment filled with empathy and support.

Clear communication is the cornerstone of any strong relationship, especially when navigating the unique challenges of ADHD. When family members understand specific symptoms and how they manifest in daily life, they're better equipped to offer you the support you need. For instance, ADHD can impact attention, making it difficult to follow conversations or instructions without drifting off. It might also lead to impulsivity, where thoughts are vocalized without a filter, potentially causing misunderstandings. Sharing these nuances with family helps them see that these behaviors aren't a reflection of your feelings toward them but rather a facet of how your brain functions.

Personal stories are powerful tools for fostering empathy and awareness. By sharing your experiences, you invite family members into your world, allowing them to walk a mile in your shoes. Talk about a day when your mind felt like a whirlwind or a time you misplaced something important despite having just seen it moments ago. These anecdotes provide context, turning abstract concepts into tangible experiences. They offer a window into your reality, helping family members understand that ADHD isn't just a label but a lived experience that shapes your interactions with the world.

Effective communication strategies can transform how you convey your needs and challenges. Start by using "I" statements to express feelings and needs, such as "I feel overwhelmed when I can't find my keys because it disrupts my routine." This approach focuses on your experience rather than assigning blame, inviting understanding rather than defensiveness. Regular family meetings can also serve as a platform to discuss organizational goals and address concerns. These gatherings provide a safe space to voice struggles and brainstorm solutions collectively, fostering a sense of teamwork and shared responsibility.

Helping family members understand ADHD can significantly reduce misunderstandings and improve relationships. When everyone is on the same page, it's easier to approach challenges collaboratively rather than contentiously. With knowledge comes compassion, allowing family members to see past the behaviors to the person behind them. This understanding paves the way for collaborative problem-solving, where together, you can craft solutions to consider everyone's needs and strengths.

Maintaining open lines of communication requires ongoing effort and dialogue. It's not a one-time conversation but a continuous exchange of thoughts and feelings. Encourage family members to ask questions and express their concerns, ensuring communication flows both ways. Consider setting aside time for regular check-ins, where everyone can share updates and address any emerging issues. Remember, the goal is to create a supportive environment where everyone feels heard and valued.

Interactive Element: Family Communication Reflection

Set aside time for a family meeting and invite members to share their thoughts and feelings about living with ADHD. Encourage using "I" statements and active listening, where each person reflects on what they've heard before responding. This exercise can help build empathy and understanding, laying the groundwork for a more supportive home environment.

Communicating openly and educating those closest to you creates a more understanding environment and strengthens the bonds that hold your family together. This chapter fosters an atmosphere of empathy by encouraging open communication, understanding, and shared problem-solving, helping you work together to craft practical and supportive solutions that strengthen your family connections.

10.1 Collaborative Cleaning: Engaging Partners and Kids

Imagine turning cleaning from a solo chore into a lively family affair. Collaborative cleaning not only makes tidying up more manageable but also nurtures a sense of teamwork and shared responsibility in the household. Involving family members in cleaning tasks transforms what might feel like a mundane obligation into an opportunity for togetherness. Assigning age-appropriate tasks ensures everyone feels included and capable. Young children can handle simple tasks like sorting laundry or picking up toys, while older kids might tackle vacuuming or organizing shelves. It's about matching tasks to abilities so everyone can contribute meaningfully without feeling overwhelmed.

To keep engagement high, consider rotating chores regularly, which helps prevent monotony and allows each family member to learn and master different skills. One week, your partner might be responsible for the kitchen while you handle the living room; the next week, you swap roles. This rotation maintains interest and builds empathy as each person gains an appreciation for the diverse tasks involved in maintaining a household. Establishing designated times for family clean-ups can transform how you approach household chores. Choose a time that works for everyone, perhaps on a weekend morning, and embark on a collective effort to tidy the home. When cleaning becomes a shared activity, it feels less like a burden and more like a communal ritual.

Transforming chores into enjoyable experiences can change the way your family views cleaning. Start by creating a family cleaning playlist filled with upbeat music everyone loves. Music has a magical way of turning even the most mundane tasks into something fun. As tunes fill the air, you might find yourselves singing along or even breaking into a spontaneous dance party while sweeping the floor. The power of music lies in its ability to lift spirits and make time fly, turning cleaning into a source of joy rather than an unwelcome chore.

Another strategy involves establishing a reward system for completed tasks. Rewards don't need to be extravagant; sometimes, the promise of a family movie night or an ice cream outing is motivation enough. Consider using a points system where each completed chore earns points toward a collective family treat. This approach not only incentivizes participation but also instills a sense of accomplishment and teamwork. The focus shifts from just getting the job done to enjoying the process and celebrating achievements together.

Remember, the goal of collaborative cleaning is not just to maintain a tidy home but to strengthen family bonds. Engaging in these activities together encourages communication and cooperation, teaching valuable life skills while building a sense of unity. It's about creating an environment where each family member feels valued and appreciated for their contributions. As you integrate these strategies into your routine, cleaning becomes less about the tasks and more about the connections forged in the process. The family that cleans together not only keeps a tidy home but also cultivates a spirit of collaboration and camaraderie.

10.2 Creating a Harmonious Home: Setting Boundaries

Imagine the comfort of a home where everyone knows their own space, where personal zones are respected, and where shared areas are maintained with mutual understanding. Establishing boundaries in shared spaces acts as a roadmap, guiding family members toward harmonious interactions while keeping both private and communal areas organized and functional. When you designate personal zones for each family member, it's not just about physical space, it's about creating emotional safety and freedom. A child might have a reading nook or a corner filled with art supplies, while a partner might have their part of the garage for hobbies. These zones allow personal expression and a sense of ownership. In shared areas like the living room or kitchen, establishing rules can help maintain order. Perhaps it's as simple as agreeing that shoes are left by the door or the dishes go in the dishwasher right after meals. These agreements keep common areas pleasant and functional for everyone.

Implementing and respecting boundaries requires clear communication and consistency. Visual cues like labels or signs are effective tools. They're subtle reminders that reinforce boundaries without constant verbal reminders. A label on a bin might read "Dad's Tools," or a sign on a door might indicate "Quiet Zone" during certain hours. These cues help everyone understand and respect each other's space. Regular discussions are crucial to reassess and adjust boundaries as needed. Families grow and change, and so do their needs. Holding a monthly family meeting to discuss what's working and what isn't can help maintain harmony. These discussions are opportunities to express needs and negotiate changes, ensuring that boundaries continue to serve everyone well.

Boundaries play a vital role in fostering independence and respect within the family. They encourage self-reliance by allowing individuals the autonomy to manage their spaces and responsibilities. A teenager learning to keep their room tidy is developing life skills that will serve them well beyond the family home. Boundaries also promote mutual respect and understanding among family members. When everyone knows and respects the rules, it reduces conflict and creates an environment where everyone feels valued. The respect for personal space extends to respect for personal time and emotions, nurturing an atmosphere of empathy and consideration.

Effective boundary-setting practices vary but share common principles. For example, dedicating specific shelves to different family members in a kitchen can prevent squabbles over space. Each person knows where their snacks or ingredients are, reducing friction. In living areas, establishing quiet hours can help balance the needs of those who thrive in silence and those who enjoy lively conversations. Post the hours on a family bulletin board as a gentle reminder for everyone. In bedrooms, encouraging the personalization of space allows individuals to express themselves and take pride in maintaining their areas.

Boundaries aren't about restriction but about creating a framework that considers everyone's needs. They provide the structure necessary for a home to thrive, balancing individual freedom with communal harmony. When boundaries are respected, they become a source of strength, helping each family member feel secure and understood. This balance makes a home a sanctuary, a place where everyone can unwind and connect without the chaos of constant contention.

10.3 Finding External Support: Groups and Communities

Living with ADHD can sometimes feel like navigating a maze without a map. While family support forms a crucial foundation, adding external support networks can provide a much-needed boost. These networks offer fresh perspectives and strategies that complement what you're already doing at home. Imagine sitting in a room where everyone just gets it. That's the power of these groups. They offer emotional support and validation, reminding you you're not alone in this journey. Sometimes, hearing someone else's story can shine a light on your own path, offering new ways to tackle familiar challenges.

There are various types of support networks available for individuals with ADHD, each catering to different needs and preferences. Local ADHD support groups or meetup events provide a space for face-to-face interaction, allowing you to connect with people in your community who understand what you're going through. These groups often meet regularly, offering a consistent source of support and solidarity. If in-person meetings aren't feasible, online forums and communities focused on ADHD present an excellent alternative. Platforms like these offer the flexibility to engage at your convenience, connecting you with a global network of individuals who share similar experiences. Look for an online space like a Facebook group or a specialized ADHD forum filled with people eager to share advice, resources, and encouragement.

Engaging in support networks can lead to personal growth and better coping mechanisms. When you participate in these communities, you open yourself up to a wealth of shared experiences with like-minded people. Listening to others' journeys can provide insights and strategies you might not have considered. It's like having access to a collective brain trust, where everyone's unique perspective adds value. Building friendships and connections with others who understand ADHD challenges helps alleviate feelings of isolation. These bonds foster a sense of belonging, making it easier to navigate the ups and downs of daily life. As you share your own stories, you contribute to the community's richness, creating a cycle of support and growth.

Finding and engaging with supportive communities doesn't have to be daunting. Start by researching local community centers or mental health organizations to discover support groups they might host. These organizations often have resources or can point you in the right direction. Exploring social media groups and online platforms dedicated to ADHD is another excellent way to find supportive communities. Search for "ADHD support groups" on your preferred platform, and you'll likely find numerous options to choose from. It's important to find a group that resonates with you, where you feel comfortable and understood. Take your time to explore different options, and don't hesitate to try out a few until you find the right fit.

As we wrap up our exploration of engaging with family and support networks, remember that building a support system is like crafting a safety net. It's there to catch you when things get tough and to lift you up when you're ready to soar. In the next chapter, we'll delve into maintaining motivation and momentum, harnessing these newfound connections to fuel your journey toward a more organized and fulfilling life. Together, we'll continue to forge a path where ADHD becomes not just a challenge but a part of your strength.

Chapter 11

Inspiration and Success Stories

Have you ever watched a movie where the protagonist faces seemingly insurmountable chaos, only to turn things around with an unexpected twist of ingenuity? It's a narrative that resonates deeply with someone living with ADHD, navigating through the turmoil of disorganization to emerge victorious. In this chapter, we dive into real-life stories of individuals who have transformed their lives from chaos to order, using innovative strategies that inspire and empower. These stories encompass diverse backgrounds and challenges, reflecting the unique ways people with ADHD have found their path to organization.

Meet Alex, a young professional who juggled the demands of a corporate job with a bustling home life. After being diagnosed with ADHD, Alex felt overwhelmed by the clutter that seemed to accumulate both at work and at home. Paperwork piled up, and digital reminders went unnoticed. But Alex turned things around with a strategic approach. Alex created a visual map of responsibilities by adopting color-coded systems for managing tasks. Each color represented a different priority, making focusing on what truly mattered easier. Coupling this with technology, Alex set up digital alerts for meetings and deadlines, ensuring nothing slipped through the cracks. The transformation was profound. Alex experienced the joy and relief of reaching organizational milestones, finally feeling in control of work and home life.

In another corner of the world, there's Mia, a parent balancing a household with multiple ADHD family members. For Mia, managing the chaos of daily life required creativity and patience. The initial feelings of frustration were intense, with toys, school supplies, and household items scattered everywhere. Mia decided to turn organization into a family affair. Mia fostered a sense of responsibility and teamwork by involving each family member in the process. One unique solution was assigning each child a "clutter companion"—a tangible reminder to keep their space tidy. This simple yet effective strategy turned cleaning into a game, making it fun and engaging. Seeing the joy on her kids' faces when they reached organizational goals was a testament to the power of collaboration and innovation.

Now, let's step into the life of Sam, a college student living in shared housing. The challenges of maintaining personal space in a communal environment were daunting. Sam initially felt overwhelmed by the constant movement and noise, which made focusing on studies difficult. But Sam's ingenuity shone through. Sam created a personalized system that organized study materials and personal items by using visual cues, like colorful sticky notes and labeled storage bins. Utilizing noise-canceling headphones during study periods kept noises to a minimum, aiding his ability to concentrate. This approach helped Sam manage physical clutter and provided a mental framework to tackle academic responsibilities. The sense of accomplishment and relief was palpable as Sam navigated college life with newfound confidence and clarity.

Then there's Jamie, an ambitious entrepreneur juggling the complexities of running a business from a home office. The blending of work and personal life often led to chaos, with important documents lost among household clutter and an overwhelming list of tasks. Jamie's turning point came with embracing technology as an organizing ally. Using a task management app, Jamie created clear distinctions between professional and personal responsibilities, prioritizing tasks and deadlines visually. A shared calendar app helped streamline household schedules, ensuring everyone was on the same page. By transitioning to cloud-based file storage, Jamie organized critical documents and made them easily accessible, reducing stress and saving time. These tools allowed Jamie to transform a chaotic space into an efficient, balanced environment.

These narratives illustrate that the journey from chaos to order is not just about physical transformation but also an emotional one. The initial overwhelm and frustration give way to joy and relief as individuals find strategies that work for them. From color-coded systems to collaborative family efforts and visual cues to technological aids, each story offers a unique perspective on overcoming the challenges of ADHD. These real-life examples remind us that organization is within reach for everyone with creativity, persistence, and the right tools.

Interactive Element: Reflect on Your Journey

Take a moment to reflect on your own organizing journey. Consider the challenges you've faced or are currently facing and the emotions tied to them. What unique strategies could you adopt from these stories? Write down two or three ideas that resonate with you, and think about how you might apply them in your own life. Use this reflection as a stepping stone toward your transformation, turning chaos into a manageable and fulfilling path.

11.1 Case Studies: Successful Organizing with ADHD

James and Emma constantly clashed over their shared living space, which had become a source of frustration and tension. Despite excelling in demanding jobs and maintaining active social lives, they needed help with disorganization at home. Clutter piled up on kitchen counters, closets overflowed, and misplaced items added stress to their daily routines. Arguments often broke out as each blamed the other for the mess. Simple tasks, like finding keys or preparing dinner, became stressful ordeals. The chaos wasn't just disrupting their home life; it was straining their relationship. They realized they needed to address the issue together before it caused further damage.

They started by having an honest conversation about how the disorganization affected their lives. They acknowledged their shared responsibility and committed to tackling the problem as a team. They introduced weekly family meetings to bring structure and collaboration into their efforts. These meetings gave them a platform to discuss frustrations, celebrate progress, and adjust plans as needed. By aligning their expectations and dividing tasks, they created a system that restored balance to their home.

During the meetings, they assigned responsibilities based on their strengths. James took charge of meal planning and kitchen organization, enjoying the opportunity to bring order to the heart of their home. Emma focused on organizing the living room and shared storage spaces, finding satisfaction in creating a sense of order. This division of labor created ownership and accountability, which reduced arguments and strengthened their teamwork.

To keep their momentum, they incorporated practical tools. They used visual timers to focus on one task at a time, breaking larger projects into manageable intervals. Time blocking helped them schedule cleaning sessions without disrupting work or leisure. They also relied on shared digital calendars and task management apps to stay coordinated and track progress.

These strategies transformed their home into a functional and peaceful space. James and Emma's communication improved as they worked together, and the reduced clutter brought them a sense of calm. Their home no longer fueled arguments; it reflected their shared effort and mutual respect. By addressing the challenges constructively, they strengthened their relationship and proved that even small changes could lead to profound improvements.

In another case, we have Lisa. She sought the guidance of an ADHD coach to tackle her personal organizing challenges. She struggled to maintain consistent cleaning routines, and her home often mirrored her chaotic thoughts. Piles of laundry and scattered papers created a constant sense of disarray. Her coach worked with her to identify specific hurdles, like her tendency to get easily distracted and her lack of a structured cleaning approach.

Together, they developed a routine that used visual cues and reminders to keep Lisa on track. They tested various techniques and discovered that a visual cleaning schedule worked best for her. Using colorful charts, they broke down tasks into manageable steps, assigning each day a specific focus, such as tidying the bedroom or organizing the kitchen. This structure gave Lisa a clear direction, easing the overwhelm that had previously stalled her progress. With her coach's encouragement, Lisa celebrated small victories, which reinforced positive habits and boosted her motivation.

The outcomes for both James, Emma, and Lisa were transformative. For the couple, improved communication and a more organized living environment led to a happier, more peaceful home life. They found that by working together and using ADHD-friendly strategies, they could maintain a balance between their personal and shared spaces. Meanwhile, Lisa experienced a significant reduction in stress and increased productivity. Her home became a sanctuary rather than a source of anxiety, allowing her to focus on personal and professional goals with newfound clarity. These case studies highlight how tailored strategies can turn the chaos of ADHD into an opportunity for growth and harmony, demonstrating that organization is achievable with the right tools and support.

11.2 Lessons Learned: Applying Strategies in Everyday Life

In navigating the world of organization with ADHD, flexibility stands out as a cornerstone. It's like learning to dance in the rain instead of waiting for the storm to pass. The success stories and case studies we've explored highlight one universal truth: rigid systems often crumble under the weight of real life. Consider individuals' varied approaches, each tailored to their unique circumstances. Flexibility in organizing approaches is not just beneficial but necessary. The ability to pivot and adapt when a strategy doesn't quite fit keeps the momentum going. This could mean adjusting a cleaning schedule to align with your energy peaks or redesigning a workspace to suit your changing needs better. It's about being open to change and willing to try new things when the old ones stop working.

Persistence and patience are your allies in this endeavor. Think of them as the steady hands guiding you through the chaos. Achieving organizational goals doesn't happen overnight, especially when ADHD is part of the equation. The stories shared earlier reflect this journey of persistence. There were moments of frustration and setbacks, but each small step forward was a victory in itself. It's important to remember that every effort, no matter how small, contributes to the larger picture. This patience with oneself, coupled with a persistent attitude, transforms challenges into stepping stones. It's akin to navigating through a labyrinth, where each step, no matter how small, guides us closer to the exit. The commitment to keep going, even when progress seems slow, ultimately results in meaningful change.

Adaptable techniques are the unsung heroes of successful organization. The beauty of these strategies lies in their ability to fit seamlessly into different lifestyles and needs. Simplifying organizing tasks through routine habit integration is one such technique that involves embedding small organizational tasks into existing routines, making them a natural part of your day. Imagine tidying up your workspace while waiting for your morning coffee to brew or sorting mail during a TV commercial break. These small actions, when repeated, build a habit that requires less conscious effort over time.

Additionally, leveraging community support and accountability can provide the encouragement needed to stay on track. Joining a group or having an accountability partner can offer motivation and a sense of connection. Sharing goals and celebrating successes with others can reinforce your commitment to organization.

Fostering a mindset of experimentation and flexibility is essential. It's about giving yourself the freedom to explore different methods and find what resonates with you. Testing various digital tools for task management is a great place to start. There are countless apps designed to help with organization, each offering unique features. Whether it's an app that gamifies chores or one that provides visual reminders, exploring these tools can help you discover what works best for you.

Additionally, adapting organizing strategies based on personal energy levels can significantly impact your productivity. Pay attention to when you feel most alert and focused, and schedule organizing tasks during those times. This alignment with your natural rhythms can make tasks feel less daunting and more manageable.

Ongoing learning is the key to continuous improvement and adaptation. The landscape of organization is ever-evolving, with new resources and techniques emerging all the time. Engaging with these new organizing resources and literature keeps your strategies fresh and relevant. Consider attending workshops or joining support groups to connect with others facing similar challenges. These settings provide opportunities to learn from others' experiences and gain new insights. The exchange of ideas in these communities can spark creativity and inspire new approaches. It's about maintaining a mindset of curiosity and openness, where every day offers a chance to learn something new. This continuous learning enhances your organizational skills and contributes to personal growth, shaping a more balanced and fulfilling life.

11.3 Celebrating Success: Reflecting on Achievements

Celebrating your organizing successes is essential for maintaining momentum. Recognizing achievements, whether big or small, plays a crucial role in sustaining motivation. Have you ever noticed how simply acknowledging your hard work can lift your spirits and push you to keep going? One effective way to visualize your progress is by creating a "success board." Think of it as a living gallery of achievements, where you pin photos, notes, or tokens of each victory. This board is a testament to your journey, constantly reminding you of how far you've come. It's a space where you can see your efforts come to life, inspiring you to tackle future challenges with renewed vigor. Sharing these accomplishments with supportive communities can also amplify your sense of achievement. Whether it's an online group or friends who cheer you on, celebrating together strengthens bonds and builds a network of encouragement.

There are countless creative ways to celebrate your achievements, each one adding a personal touch to your victories. Imagine hosting a small gathering to showcase your newly organized space. Inviting friends to admire your work highlights your accomplishment and fills your home with positive energy. It's a chance to gather with those who have supported you, sharing the joy of transformation. Or perhaps you prefer a quieter celebration, like treating yourself to a relaxing day off after completing a major project. This intentional pause allows you to recharge and reflect, savoring the satisfaction of a job well done. These celebrations, whether grand or intimate, serve as milestones that mark your progress, reinforcing the positive changes you've made.

Reflecting on your journey and the lessons learned along the way is equally important. Take time to assess your progress and set new goals for the future. Journaling can be a powerful tool for this reflection. Write about your organizing experiences, noting the challenges you faced and the strategies that worked best. This practice helps solidify your achievements and provides insights for future endeavors. As you look back, you may find patterns that guide your next steps, helping you refine your approach. Setting new objectives based on past successes ensures that your organizing efforts continue to evolve, adapting to your changing needs and circumstances.

Continual growth and improvement are the heartbeats of personal development and organization. Embrace the ongoing nature of this process, understanding that organizing is not a one-time task but a lifelong pursuit. Revisit your goals regularly, adjusting and refining your strategies as you learn and grow. This adaptability allows you to respond to life's changes with grace and strength. Lifelong learning also plays a vital role in this journey. Stay curious and open to new ideas, whether it's trying fresh organizing techniques or attending workshops to enhance your skills. This commitment to growth keeps your organizing efforts fresh and practical, ensuring that they continue to support your life in meaningful ways.

As you celebrate your achievements and reflect on your journey, remember that every step forward showcases your resilience and determination. Your progress is a mosaic of challenges conquered and victories earned, brought together through creativity and perseverance. Each milestone draws you closer to a home and life that aligns with your values and aspirations. With every accomplishment, you move closer to balance and fulfillment, ready to embrace the possibilities ahead.

Chapter 12

Practical Tools and Resources

Picture starting your day with a clear plan in hand, knowing exactly what you need to do and when. Living with ADHD can often feel like navigating a whirlwind of distractions, where important tasks easily slip through the cracks. That's where the simple yet powerful checklist comes into play—a beacon of organization in the midst of chaos. Checklists are more than just lists; they're structured roadmaps that provide direction and clarity. They help transform a scattered schedule into a series of achievable steps. Imagine a daily to-do list that highlights your priorities, helping you focus on what truly matters, or a weekly cleaning checklist that breaks down chores into smaller, manageable actions, reducing the sense of overwhelm.

Checklists cater to various areas of life, from grocery shopping to project planning. When it comes to grocery shopping, organizing lists by store sections can streamline your trip, ensuring everything is remembered and saving you time. For project planning, step-by-step actions in a checklist offer a clear path forward, reducing the mental load of figuring out what comes next. The beauty of checklists lies in their versatility, adapting to your unique needs and preferences. Whether you're planning a big work project or simply trying to stay on top of daily errands, checklists can be a game-changer.

Choosing between digital and paper checklists often comes down to personal preference and lifestyle. Digital checklists, like those offered in apps like TickTick and Sunsama, have the added benefit of reminder features and easy editing. They can be accessed on multiple devices, ensuring your list is always at your fingertips. On the other hand, paper checklists provide a tactile experience that many find satisfying. The act of physically crossing off a completed task can be incredibly rewarding. Plus, they don't require a device, making them ideal for those who prefer a screen-free approach.

Maintaining and updating checklists ensures they remain practical tools. Regularly reviewing and revising lists keeps them relevant and adaptable to changes in your life. Consider using color coding to indicate task status—green for completed, yellow for in progress, and red for urgent. This visual cue provides an overview of what's done and pending. Ultimately, the key is to find a system that works for you, one that complements your lifestyle and enhances your ability to manage tasks efficiently.

Interactive Element: Checklist Reflection Exercise

Take a moment to reflect on your current use of checklists. Are they serving you well, or is there room for improvement? Jot down areas where you feel a checklist could enhance your organization—be it daily tasks, work projects, or personal goals. Consider experimenting with both digital and paper formats to find your preference. Use color coding to categorize tasks and see how it impacts your productivity. This exercise aims to refine your approach, ensuring your checklist becomes an indispensable part of your organizational toolkit.

12.1 Creating Your Personalized Planner System

Creating a personalized planner can transform how you manage your day-to-day tasks, making them feel less like chores and more like stepping stones toward your aspirations. Start by selecting a format that suits your rhythm—whether it's a daily planner for detailed scheduling, a weekly one for broader overviews, or a monthly layout to capture the big picture. Each format offers unique advantages, so consider what fits your lifestyle best.

Incorporate personal goals and priorities into your planner, turning it into a visual representation of your ambitions. This isn't just about jotting down tasks; it's about mapping out a path that leads you to where you want to be.

A personalized planner does more than keep you organized; it enhances your productivity and focus. By aligning with your routines and schedules, it becomes a tool that works with you, not against you. Imagine the ease of having a dedicated place for habit trackers that help you build and maintain routines or sections for notes and reflections where you can jot down thoughts, ideas, and insights. These components make your planner more than just a calendar; they turn it into a companion that supports your growth and progress. It's about creating a system that acknowledges and adapts to your needs, providing both structure and flexibility.

Maintaining your planner is vital to keeping it functional and effective. Regularly set aside time for planner reviews, a quiet moment to assess what's working and what needs tweaking. This practice ensures your planner remains relevant and aligned with your evolving life. Be open to adapting the layout as your circumstances change. Maybe a new job demands a shift in focus, or personal goals require a new approach. Your planner should reflect these shifts, evolving with you rather than becoming stagnant. By keeping it up-to-date, you ensure it continues to serve its purpose as a guide and motivator.

Creating a personalized planner is more than just managing your schedule; it's about creating a tool that reflects your unique needs and aligns your daily routines with your bigger goals.

12.2 Visual Aids: Using Charts and Infographics

Imagine standing in front of a wall covered in sticky notes, each one a different color representing various tasks, ideas, and reminders. When you have ADHD, visual aids transform abstract thoughts into something tangible. They simplify complex information, making it easier to grasp and remember. A flowchart, for example, can be very helpful in decision-making processes. It lays out each step clearly, helping you visualize paths and outcomes and making those overwhelming decisions feel more manageable. Infographics, on the other hand, summarize key concepts in a way that's both engaging and easy to digest. They turn dry information into a visual feast, pulling you in and keeping your attention.

Visual aids come in many forms, each serving a unique purpose. A color-coded calendar, for instance, not only schedules tasks but also provides a visual cue for priorities. Each color signifies an area of your life—work, personal, health—and helps you balance them with ease. Visual progress trackers are another powerful tool. They offer a sense of achievement, marking milestones and illustrating your journey towards a goal. Whether it's a weight loss chart or a savings tracker, these tools provide a visual reminder of how far you've come and how much closer you are to your objectives.

The benefits of using visual aids extend beyond mere organization. They aid in memory retention, turning fleeting thoughts into lasting impressions. By transforming abstract tasks into concrete visual plans, you engage more senses, which helps solidify information in your mind. Visual aids also enhance engagement, inviting you to interact with your plans rather than observe them passively. This active participation can boost motivation and keep you invested in your tasks and goals.

Creating effective visual aids involves a few key considerations. First, clarity and simplicity are paramount. Use software or templates that allow you to design with precision and ease. Avoid cluttering your visuals with excessive details; focus on the core elements that convey your message. Remember, the goal is to enhance understanding, not overwhelm you with information. Choose colors and fonts that are easy on the eyes and align with the tone of your content.

12.3 DIY Organizing Tools: Cost-Effective Solutions

DIY organizing tools offer a wallet-friendly solution and a chance to tailor your storage to fit your unique space and needs. Start by looking around your home for items that can be repurposed. An old shoebox, for example, can be transformed into a drawer divider, perfect for tidying up that chaotic sock collection. With just a bit of cardboard and creativity, you can create compartments that neatly separate your belongings, turning clutter into order. Similarly, crafting a wall-mounted mail organizer from recycled wood or cardboard can help keep those pesky paper piles at bay, giving your entryway a cleaner look.

Crafting your own organizers isn't just about saving money; it's about customization. When you make something yourself, you have complete control over its size, shape, and functionality. Tailor these creations to fit the nooks and crannies of your home, addressing specific needs that store-bought solutions often overlook. This personal touch ensures that your organizing tools serve their purpose and blend seamlessly with your decor and lifestyle. The process of creating these tools can also be incredibly satisfying. It's a chance to flex your creative muscles and take ownership of your space in a new way.

A little planning goes a long way to embark on a successful DIY organizing project. Begin by gathering the necessary materials and tools. Whether it's scissors, glue, or a measuring tape, having everything at hand prevents interruptions and makes the process smoother. Following step-by-step guides or tutorials can also be invaluable, especially when tackling a new project. These resources offer guidance and inspiration, helping you bring your vision to life. Keep in mind that the goal is to create something functional and durable, so take your time and enjoy the process.

12.4 Printable Resources for Continuous Motivation

Picture this: you wake up, grab your morning coffee, and see an inspirational quote on your fridge that sparks a small flame of motivation inside of you. These printables are more than just pieces of paper; they're daily companions that keep you focused on your goals. They're like little coaches, cheering you on from the sidelines. Whether it's a quote reminding you of your strength or a worksheet guiding you through your dreams, these resources provide a tangible source of encouragement.

Imagine having a monthly habit tracker on your desk, each filled square a testament to your commitment. Or a meal planning template that simplifies your week, helping you make mindful choices without the usual stress. These printables anchor you, providing stability amidst life's unpredictable tides. They're practical, sure, but they also foster a deeper engagement with your tasks. By physically interacting with your goals, whether through jotting down a new idea or coloring in a completed task, you're not just planning—you're participating actively in your success.

Integrating these printables into your life can be simple. Pin them up in places you frequent—like the bathroom mirror or next to your monitor—keeping your goals front and center. This visibility ensures you won't forget them; instead, they will become part of your daily routine. Regularly update and replace them to reflect current goals, keeping your motivation fresh and relevant. It's about creating a dynamic environment where your objectives live and breathe, constantly evolving alongside you. These printables do more than organize; they inspire, remind, and celebrate each step you take.

12.5 Building Your Support Network: Finding Help and Accountability

A support network is so important when you're navigating the challenges of ADHD. Having a circle of people who not only understand your struggles but will always be there cheering you on. It can transform your journey, providing both motivation and accountability. Emotional support from family and friends is invaluable, offering a shoulder to lean on during tough times. They remind you that you're not alone and that your struggles are seen and understood. Moreover, guidance from professional organizers or coaches can bring clarity and structure to your life. They offer strategies tailored to your needs, helping you create systems that work for you.

Building this network requires some effort, but the rewards are worth it. Start by seeking out online communities or forums where people share similar experiences. These spaces can be a treasure trove of tips and encouragement. Local workshops or meet-ups are another great avenue. They offer face-to-face connections, creating opportunities to exchange ideas and support. In these environments, you'll find people who understand your journey because they're on one, too.

Accountability partners provide invaluable benefits. Having someone to check in with regularly keeps you on track, ensuring your goals remain focused. Discussing progress with a trusted partner adds a layer of commitment, transforming intentions into actions. Openly sharing challenges creates a bond, fostering a sense of mutual support and accountability. Together, you can celebrate your wins, big and small, reinforcing each other's achievements.

Proactive engagement with your support network enhances its value. Offer advice and encouragement to others, cultivating a mutually beneficial relationship. This mutual support fosters personal growth and enriches the network, creating a vibrant, dynamic space where everyone thrives.

12.6 Continuing Your Journey: Embracing a Lifetime of Organization

Organization is a lifelong adventure—one that evolves as you grow, presenting new challenges and opportunities at every turn. This journey isn't about reaching a final destination but embracing continuous growth and learning. Organization is a skill that thrives on adaptability; staying open to new techniques and ideas. As life shifts, so should your methods, ensuring they remain relevant and effective. Regularly evaluating your systems allows you to refine them, discarding what no longer serves you and adopting practices that enhance your life. Whether it's a new app, a fresh approach to time management, or a simple tweak in your daily routine, each adjustment is a step forward.

Resilience plays a crucial role in maintaining organization. Life is unpredictable, and the ability to bounce back from setbacks is invaluable. Persistence is your ally here; it's about pushing through the days when motivation wanes and finding ways to keep going. Adaptability is equally important. Sometimes, the system you've relied on may falter, requiring you to pivot and try something new. This flexibility ensures you remain in control, even when circumstances change. Remember, it's not about perfection but progress. Each small victory builds upon the last, creating a foundation of success that supports you through more challenging times.

To keep the organization momentum alive, periodically setting new challenges and goals can be highly motivating. Change revitalizes your routine, preventing it from becoming stagnant. Perhaps it's tackling a new area of your home or adopting a fresh productivity tool. These challenges keep you engaged, fostering a sense of accomplishment as you conquer each one. Alongside these challenges, it's vital to celebrate your progress and achievements. Reflection is a powerful tool, allowing you to acknowledge how far you've come. Take time to appreciate your growth, whether through journaling about your successes or simply pausing to enjoy the order you've created. These moments of reflection reinforce your efforts, motivating you to continue pursuing a life of organized harmony.

Conclusion

As we wrap up our journey together, it's clear that understanding ADHD is more than just recognizing its challenges. It's about truly appreciating the unique cognitive patterns that come with it. This understanding is your key to unlocking effective strategies for organizing and cleaning. By being self-aware, you gain the power to tailor methods that work specifically for you. It's like having a custom-made toolkit designed to fit your lifestyle perfectly.

Throughout this book, we've explored a range of strategies and techniques that can make a real difference. Remember the 5-Minute Task Technique? It's a game-changer for breaking down overwhelming chores into bite-sized tasks. We also delved into ADHD-friendly time management strategies that help you structure your day without feeling boxed in. Habit stacking and room-by-room organization have shown how small, consistent steps build up to significant improvements. Each of these techniques is practical, effective, and ready for you to put into action.

But it's not just about tidiness. A clutter-free environment does wonders for your emotional and mental well-being. It creates space not just in your home but also in your mind. With clarity comes reduced stress, and that's a gift worth striving for. You deserve to live in a space that supports your peace of mind and happiness.

The real-life success stories shared in these pages prove that organization with ADHD is not only possible but also transformative. These stories are a testament to the power of persistence, creativity, and the right approach.

They remind us that everyone's journey is unique, yet there's a common thread of hope and achievement that runs through them all.

To keep the momentum going, take full advantage of the practical tools we've covered. Whether it's checklists, planners, or visual aids, think of these as your trusty sidekicks on this journey. Keep them within reach, adjust them to fit your style, and let them work for you as you build and sustain your organizational groove. And don't forget to dive into the bonus cleaning checklist and meal planner included with this book—they're here to make your life even easier!

And remember, organization is not a destination—it's a lifelong journey. Stay open to learning and adapting. As life changes, so should your strategies. Be curious, try new techniques, and don't be afraid to switch things up when needed.

So, why not start today? Take that first step, no matter how small it may seem. Set personal goals and use the strategies in this book as your guide to creating a more organized life. Every little step counts, and before you know it, you'll build momentum toward a more stress-free, peaceful home.

Sharing your journey can be incredibly rewarding, too. Whether through community groups, online forums, or personal reflection, your experiences can inspire and support others. You're not alone; together, we can foster an encouraging environment where everyone can thrive.

I want to express my gratitude for your commitment to this journey. It has been a privilege to support you in strengthening your organizational skills. Know that I'm cheering you on as you navigate this path, and I'm here for you every step of the way.

As you continue this journey, hold on to this inspirational note: a stress-free and organized home is within your reach with the right tools and mindset. You have everything you need to make it happen, and I believe in your ability to create the environment you dream of. Here's to the beautiful, organized future ahead!

Make a Difference with Your Review

Help Others Take the First Step

"Alone we can do so little; together we can do so much." – Helen Keller

Think about the times you've felt stuck and how much it meant when someone offered a little guidance or inspiration. Now, you have the chance to do that for someone else.

Would you take a moment to help someone like you—someone ready to embrace change but unsure where to begin?

With *Organizing and Cleaning with ADHD*, my goal is to show that creating a calm, functional home is possible, even when life feels overwhelming. But for this message to reach more people who need it, I need your help.

How your review makes an impact: Most people decide which book to buy based on reviews. A quick note from you could be the encouragement they need to take that first step. Your review might help:

- One more person break free from the stress of clutter.

- One more family create a home where everyone can thrive.

- One more individual discover strategies that truly work for their ADHD brain.

- One more life change for the better.

Want to help? It's easy:

Simply scan the QR code to share your thoughts.

Your review doesn't need to be elaborate—just sincere and heartfelt. It could inspire someone to take the first step toward creating a more organized and balanced life. If helping others resonates with you, thank you for taking the time to share your thoughts and make a meaningful impact.

With gratitude,

Avery Holland

References

ADDitude. (n.d.). *Born this way: Personal stories of life with ADHD.* ADDitude Magazine. Retrieved from https://www.additudemag.com/adhd-personal-stories-real-life-people-living-with-adhd/

ADDitude. (n.d.). *Hyperfocus: How to control your ADHD focus.* ADDitude Magazine. Retrieved from https://www.additudemag.com/slideshows/hyperfocus-for-productivity/

Advanced Psychiatry Associates. (n.d.). *5 strategies for managing ADHD clutter.* Advanced Psychiatry Associates. Retrieved from https://advancedpsychiatryassociates.com/resources/blog/adhd-clutter-management-strategies

Asana. (n.d.). *Asana: Work on big ideas, without the busywork.* Retrieved from https://asana.com

Belongly. (n.d.). *Embracing digital minimalism for mindful mental health.* Belongly. Retrieved from https://www.belongly.com/digital-minimalism-a-pathway-to-improved-mental-health-and-mindfulness/

Choosing Therapy. (n.d.). *ADHD & perfectionism: Understanding the link.* Choosing Therapy. Retrieved from https://www.choosingtherapy.com/perfectionism-adhd/

Choosing Therapy. (n.d.). *Pomodoro technique for ADHD: Why it helps & how*. Choosing Therapy. Retrieved from https://www.choosingtherapy.com/pomodoro-technique-adhd/

Cold Turkey. (n.d.). *Cold Turkey: The tough productivity app*. Retrieved from https://getcoldturkey.com

Connected Speech Pathology. (n.d.). *How to improve executive function in ADHD adults: A guide*. Connected Speech Pathology. Retrieved from https://connectedspeechpathology.com/blog/how-to-improve-executive-function-in-adhd-adults

Focus Bear. (n.d.). *ADHD cleaning checklist: Simplifying the process for a tidier home*. Focus Bear. Retrieved from https://www.focusbear.io/blog-post/adhd-cleaning-checklist-simplifying-the-process-for-a-tidier-home

Focus Bear. (n.d.). *Simple steps to create an effective ADHD cleaning schedule*. Focus Bear. Retrieved from https://www.focusbear.io/blog-post/simple-steps-to-create-an-effective-adhd-cleaning-schedule

Freedom. (n.d.). *Freedom: Block distracting websites and apps*. Retrieved from https://freedom.to

Google Workspace. (n.d.). *Filters and labels in Gmail*. Retrieved from https://support.google.com

Habitica. (n.d.). *Habitica: Gamify your life*. Retrieved from https://habitica.com

Habitrpg, Inc. (n.d.). *Habitica: Gamify your tasks* [Mobile app]. Google Play Store. Retrieved from https://play.google.com/store/apps/details?id=com.habitrpg.android.habitica&hl=en_US

JED Foundation. (n.d.). *How to reduce stress by prioritizing and getting organized*. JED Foundation. Retrieved from https://jedfoundation.org/resource/how-to-reduce-stress-by-prioritizing-and-getting-organized/

Just Mind. (n.d.). *Unveiling effective ADHD communication strategies.* Just Mind. Retrieved from https://justmind.org/adhd-communication-strategies/

Justan Organized Home. (n.d.). *6 ADHD visual tools guaranteed to make organizing easy.* Justan Organized Home. Retrieved from https://justanorganizedhome.com/adhd-visual-tools/

Llama Life. (n.d.). *What is timeboxing and why it's crucial for ADHD time management and productivity.* Llama Life. Retrieved from https://llamalife.co/blog/what-is-timeboxing-and-why-is-it-crucial-for-adhd-time-management-and-productivity-clgn7muyw66122zpfl0gosa7c

Momentum. (n.d.). *Momentum Dash: Replace new tab page.* Retrieved from https://momentumdash.com

National Center for Biotechnology Information. (n.d.). *The neurobiological basis of ADHD.* PubMed Central. Retrieved from https://pmc.ncbi.nlm.nih.gov/articles/PMC3016271/

Opal. (n.d.). *How Opal helps you manage ADHD and digital distractions.* Opal. Retrieved from https://www.opal.so/blog/opal-for-adhd-and-digital-distractions

Psychology Today. (2024). *From small steps to big wins: The importance of celebrating.* Empower Your Mind. Retrieved from https://www.psychologytoday.com/us/blog/empower-your-mind/202406/from-small-steps-to-big-wins-the-importance-of-celebrating

Real Simple. (n.d.). *10 expert-backed cleaning strategies if you struggle with ADHD.* Real Simple. Retrieved from https://www.realsimple.com/cleaning-strategies-for-adhd-7724706

Sabrina's Organizing. (n.d.). *Creative ways to organize tools in a closet.* Sabrina's Organizing. Retrieved from https://sabrinasorganizing.com/tool-closet-organization/

Sorted Out. (n.d.). *Bathroom organizing tips for ADHD*. Sorted Out. Retrieved from https://www.sortedout.com/bathroom-organizing-tips-for-adhd/

Streaks. (n.d.). *Streaks: The habit tracking app*. Retrieved from https://streaksapp.com

Supersavvyme. (n.d.). *4 ways that music can help you clean*. Supersavvyme. Retrieved from https://www.supersavvyme.co.uk/home/cleaning-wizard/how-music-can-help-you-clean#:~:text=When%20you%20listen%20to%20upbeat,midway%20through%20scrubbing%20the%20tub

Tiimo App. (n.d.). *ADHD, chores, and how gamification can help*. Tiimo App. Retrieved from https://www.tiimoapp.com/resource-hub/how-turning-chores-into-quests-can-make-your-neurodivergent-brain-happy#:~:text=It%20can%20benefit%20individuals%20with,be%20gamified%20for%20better%20productivity

Todoist. (n.d.). *Todoist: The to-do list to organize work and life*. Retrieved from https://todoist.com

Trello. (n.d.). *Trello: Manage any project, at work or home*. Retrieved from https://trello.com

Unroll.Me. (n.d.). *Unroll.Me: Clean up your inbox*. Retrieved from https://unroll.me

Verywell Mind. (n.d.). *Benefits of habit stacking for ADHD*. Verywell Mind. Retrieved from https://www.verywellmind.com/habit-stacking-definition-steps-benefits-for-adhd-6751145#:~:text=Habit%20stacking%20is%20one%20kind,easier%20to%20make%20them%20stick

Work Brighter. (n.d.). *ADHD apps: 14 tools that help me stay organized*. Work Brighter. Retrieved from https://workbrighter.co/adhd-apps/

Zapier. (n.d.). *3 to-do list apps that actually work with ADHD*. Zapier. Retrieved from https://zapier.com/blog/adhd-to-do-list/

www.ingramcontent.com/pod-product-compliance
Lightning Source LLC
Chambersburg PA
CBHW020029040426
42333CB00039B/706